Tracing Sight Words Worksheets
Tracing Sight Words For Kindergarten

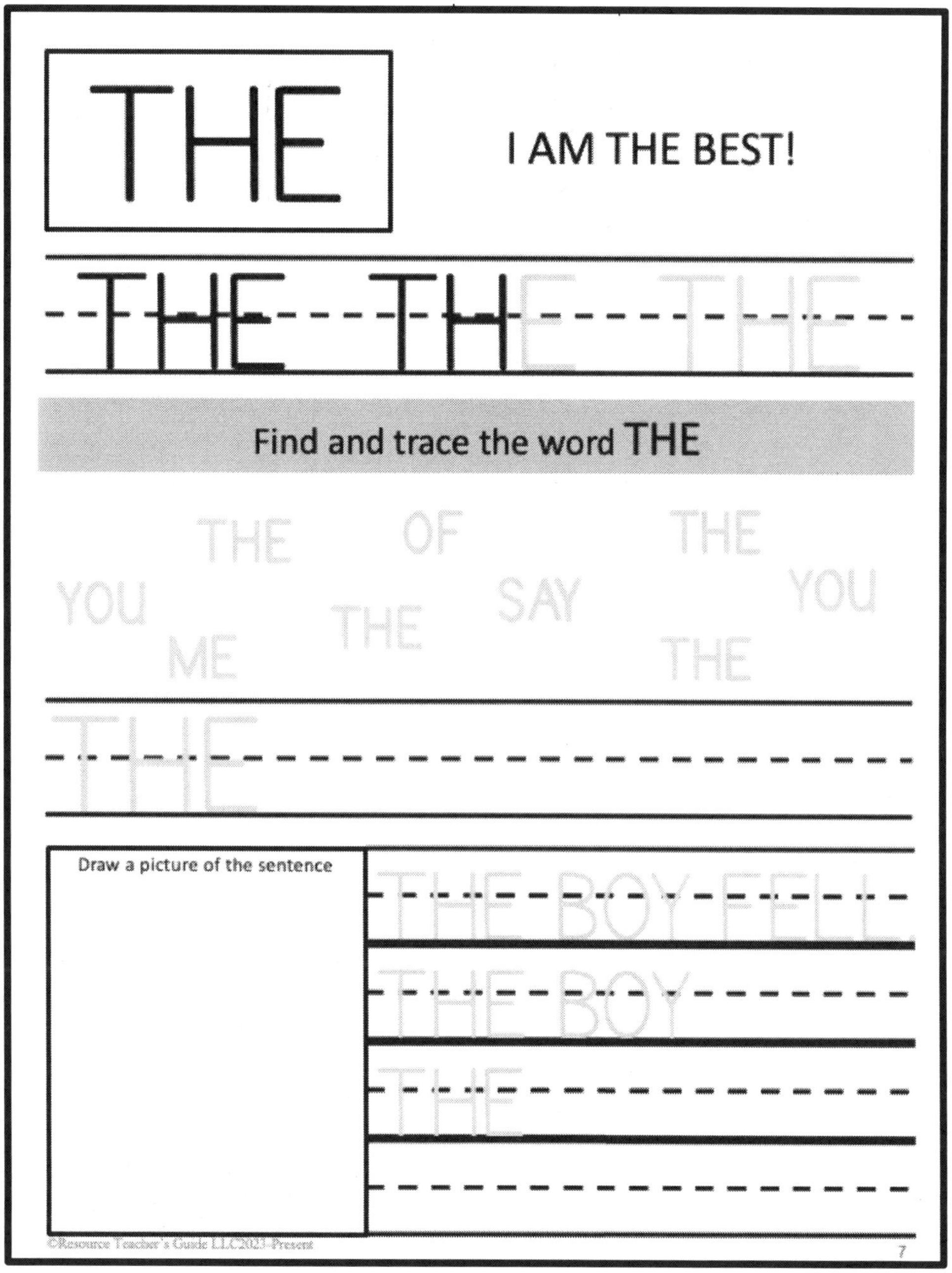

THE — I AM THE BEST!

THE TH E THE

Find and trace the word THE

THE   OF   THE
YOU   THE   SAY   YOU
ME   THE

THE

Draw a picture of the sentence

THE BOY FELL
THE BOY
THE

©Resource Teacher's Guide LLC 2023-present All rights reserved.

© Resource Teacher's Guide LLC 2023. All rights reserved.

All images created by Resource Teacher's Guide LLC. All rights reserved. No part of this publication may be reproduced, distributed, or transmitted in any form or by any means. This includes photocopying, recording, or other electronic or mechanical methods without prior permission of the publisher, except in the case of brief quotations embodied in critical reviews and other noncommercial uses permitted by copyright law.

No part of this product maybe used or reproduced for commercial use.

Contact the author:
coaches@resourceteachersguide.com

Table of Contents – 100 Sight Words

Word	Page	Word	Page	Word	Page	Word	Page	Word	Page
A	40	FOR	9	JUST	70	PUT	55	USE	107
ABOUT	106	FROM	58	KNOW	72	SAID	19	WANT	48
AGAIN	74	FUNNY	76	LIKE	44	SAW	34	WAS	25
ALL	47	GET	88	LITTLE	37	SEE	12	WE	7
AND	17	GO	15	LOOK	21	SHE	33	WERE	65
ARE	22	GOING	66	MADE	86	SO	42	WHAT	28
AS	90	GOOD	54	MAKE	94	SOME	77	WHEN	64
AT	81	HAD	89	ME	20	SOON	57	WHERE	14
AWAY	51	HAS	68	MY	8	TAKE	78	WHO	31
BE	52	HAVE	26	NEW	50	THAN	99	WOULD	102
BEEN	112	HE	32	NO	53	THAT	84	YOU	10
BUT	97	HER	56	NOT	103	THE	6	YOUR	83
BY	61	HERE	29	NOW	46	THEIR	109	REVIEW	16
CAME	45	HIM	108	OF	59	THEM	79	REVIEW	27
CAN	114	HIS	69	ON	96	THEN	67	REVIEW	38
COME	18	HOW	92	ONCE	75	THERE	36	REVIEW	49
COULD	62	I	23	OR	85	THESE	111	REVIEW	60
DID	91	IF	87	OTHER	101	THEY	35	REVIEW	71
DO	24	IN	113	OUR	43	THIS	98	REVIEW	82
EACH	100	IS	11	OUT	110	TO	13	REVIEW	93
EVERY	63	IT	95	PLAY	39	TOO	41	REVIEW	104
FIND	30	ITS	105	PLEASE	80	UNDER	73	REVIEW	115

©Resource Teacher's Guide LLC 2023-present All rights reserved.

©Resource Teacher's Guide LLC 2023-present All rights reserved.

Instructions For Use

Tracing Worksheets

1. Read the sight word and sentence
2. Trace the sight word
3. Find and trace the sight word
4. Trace the sight word then write it on your own
5. Trace the sentence
6. Trace and fill in the rest of the sentence
7. Draw a picture to match the sentence

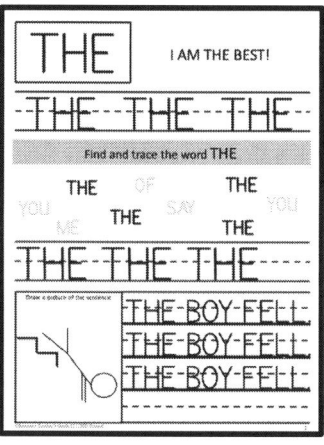

Tic-Tac-Toe Review

1. Each player picks a sight word and writes it on their line
2. Take turns writing your sight word in a spot on the tic-tac-toe
3. First to three in a row wins

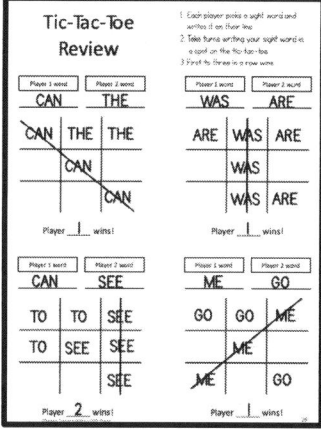

Roll and Write

1. Pick 6 sight words, write one on each line on the bottom row above the dice
2. Roll a dice and find the number on your paper
3. Write the sight word in the column
4. Whichever sight word reaches the top first wins

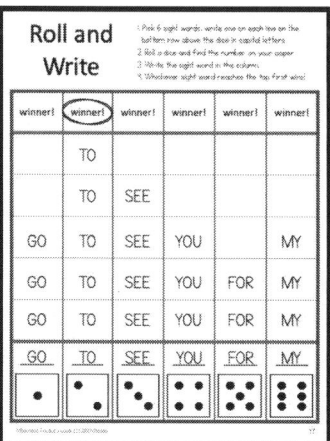

REVIEW: Word Search

1. Pick a word from the word bank
2. Find it in the word search
3. Trace it
4. Cross off the word in the word bank
5. Find them all

©Resource Teacher's Guide LLC 2023-present All rights reserved.

I AM THE BEST!

THE THE THE THE

Find and trace the word THE

THE   OF   THE
YOU   SAY   YOU
     ME   THE   THE

THE

Draw a picture of the sentence

THE BOY FELL.

THE BOY

THE

WE ALWAYS TRY.

WE WE WE

FIND AND TRACE THE WORD WE

THE FOR SAY
WE WE YOU
  CAN WE WE

WE

Draw a picture of the sentence

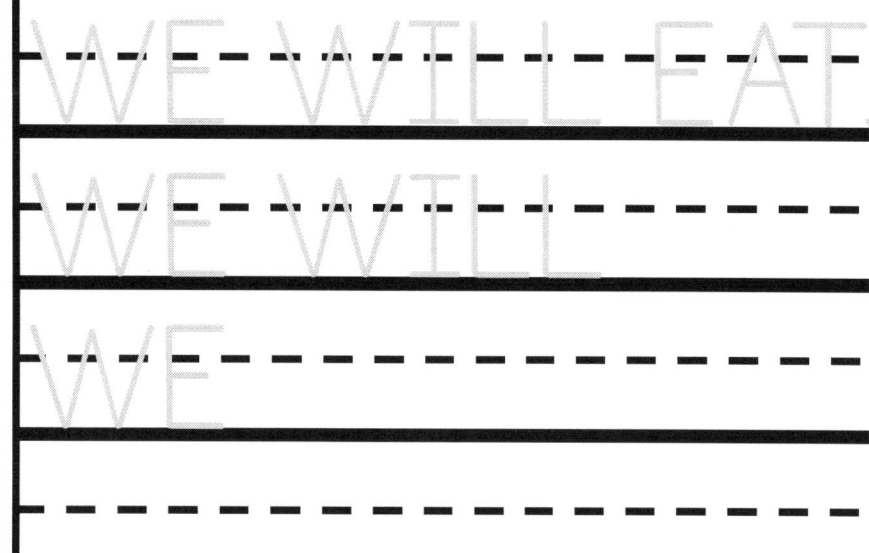

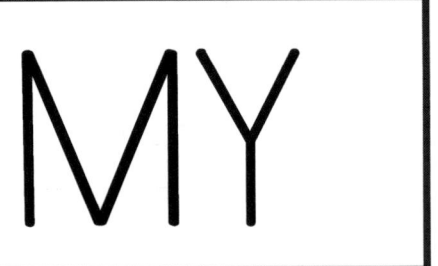

I'M GRATEFUL FOR MY MIND.

MY MY MY MY

FIND AND TRACE THE WORD MY

CAN MY DO
WE FOR MY
MY WE MY

MY

Draw a picture of the sentence

MY BUG HOPS.
MY BUG
MY

FOR

I WILL LOOK FOR GOOD IN ALL.

FOR   FOR   FOR

FIND AND TRACE THE WORD FOR

CAN   SAY   AM
FOR   FOR   FOR   DO
   YES   FOR   FOR

FOR

Draw a picture of the sentence

GO FOR IT!
GO FOR
GO

YOU

YOU ARE AMAZING!

YOU   YOU   YOU

FIND AND TRACE THE WORD YOU

FOR YOU YOU YOU DO YES AM IS YOU

YOU

Draw a picture of the sentence

I SEE YOU.

I SEE

SEE

10

IS

IT IS GOOD TO BE HERE.

IS   IS   IS   IS

FIND AND TRACE THE WORD IS

IS   THE   MY
IS   WE
   YOU   IS   IS   FOR

IS

Draw a picture of the sentence

SHE IS SAD.

SHE IS

IS

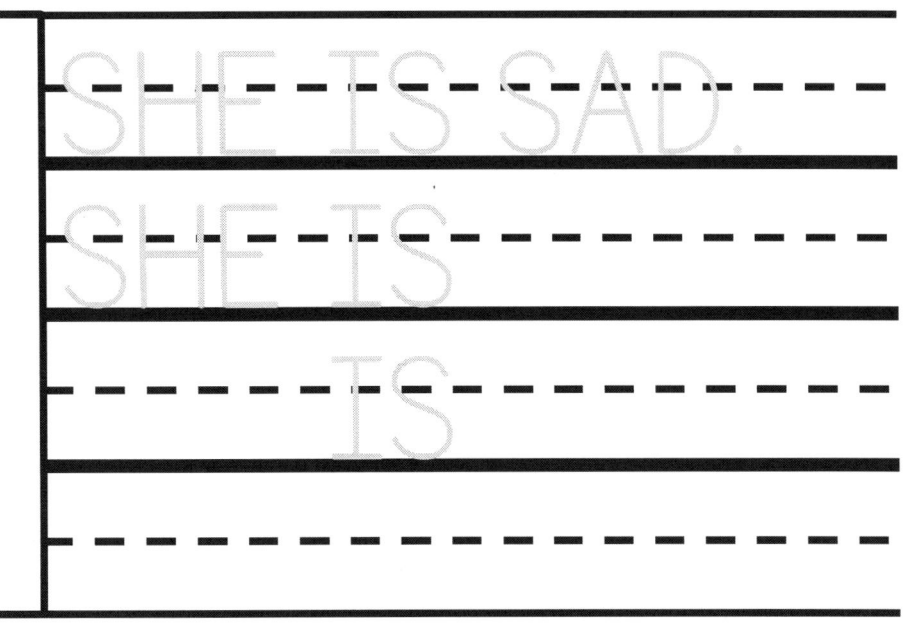

SEE

I SEE THE GOOD IN ME.

SEE   SEE   SEE   SEE

FIND AND TRACE THE WORD SEE

SEE   WE   YOU   SEE
     MY   SEE   SEE
THE   IS

SEE

Draw a picture of the sentence

SEE IT NOW?

SEE IT

SEE

TO

I CAME TO HELP!

TO TO TO TO TO

FIND AND TRACE THE WORD TO

MY	TO	TO	THE	SEE
	FOR	TO		IS
				TO

TO

Draw a picture of the sentence

GO TO BED.
GO TO
TO

WHERE

I SEE WHERE I CAN HELP.

WHERE   WHERE

FIND AND TRACE THE WORD WHERE

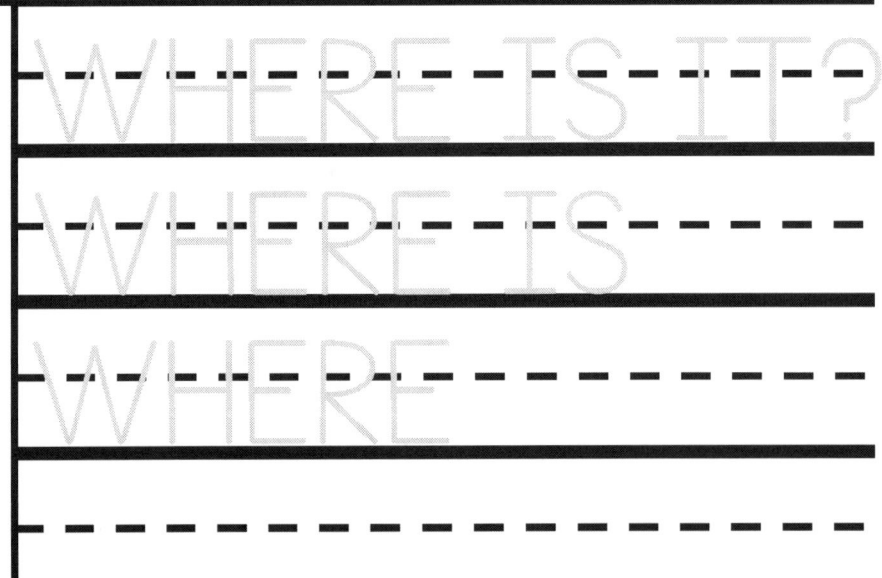

Draw a picture of the sentence

GO

GO GET THEM!

GO GO GO

FIND AND TRACE THE WORD GO

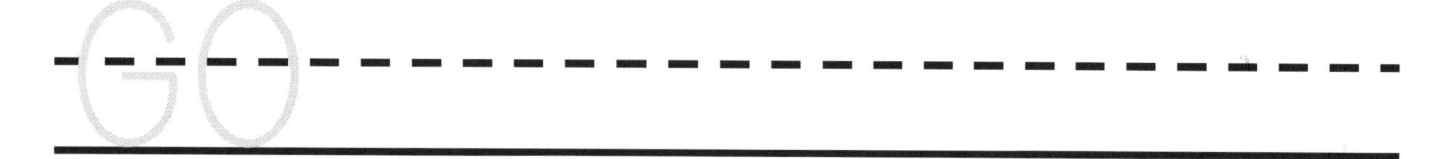

GO   YOU   GO
WHERE   IS TO   GO
GO   SEE

GO

Draw a picture of the sentence

I WILL GO.
I WILL
WILL

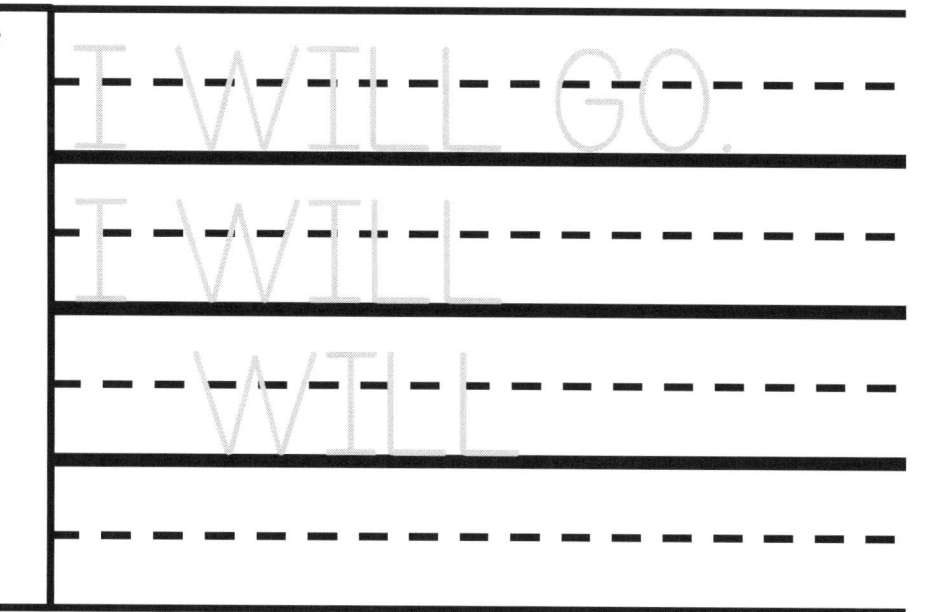

15

Roll and Write

1. Pick 6 sight words, write one on each line on the bottom row above the dice in capital letters
2. Roll a dice and find the number on your paper
3. Write the sight word in the column
4. Whichever sight word reaches the top first wins!

winner!	winner!	winner!	winner!	winner!	winner!
___ ⚀	___ ⚁	___ ⚂	___ ⚃	___ ⚄	___ ⚅

©Resource Teacher's Guide LLC 2023-Present

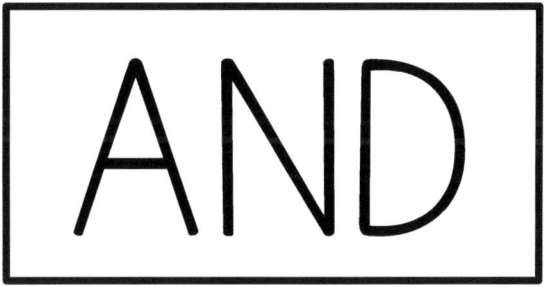

I CAN BE
HAPPY AND SAD.

AND AND AND

FIND AND TRACE THE WORD AND

TO   MY   YOU
AND   AND   AND
    SEE
  AND   GO

AND

Draw a picture of the sentence

SAND AND SEA.

SAND AND

AND

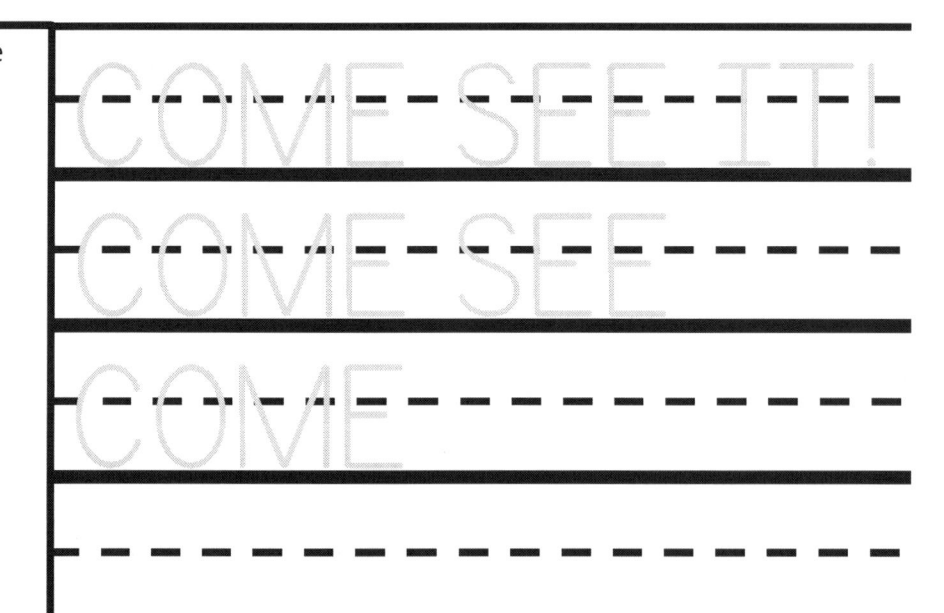

COME

COME AND PLAY WITH US!

COME   COME

FIND AND TRACE THE WORD COME

COME   TO   COME
GO   WE   THE
   WHERE   COME   COME

COME

Draw a picture of the sentence

COME SEE IT!

COME SEE

COME

SAID

I SAID YOU'RE WELCOME!

SAID   SAID

FIND AND TRACE THE WORD SAID

TO   SAID   GO
FOR   SAID   COME
    SAID   SAID
            IS

SAID

Draw a picture of the sentence

I SAID HELLO.
I SAID
SAID

ME

CAN YOU HELP ME?

ME ME ME

FIND AND TRACE THE WORD ME

WE ME ME
MY SAID FOR
ME ME WHERE
ME

ME

Draw a picture of the sentence

YOU SAVED ME!
YOU ME!
ME!

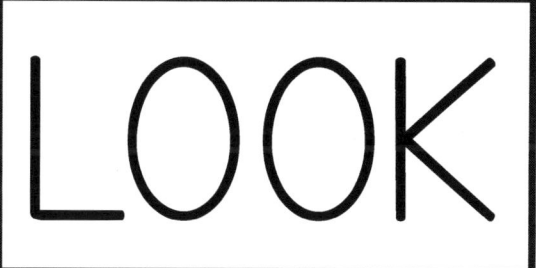

I WILL LOOK
FOR THE GOOD.

LOOK   LOOK

FIND AND TRACE THE WORD LOOK

LOOK   LOOK   FOR
LOOK   SAID   IS
AND   LOOK   COME

LOOK

Draw a picture of the sentence

I LOOK NICE!

I LOOK

LOOK

ARE

YOU ARE THE BEST!

ARE ARE ARE

FIND AND TRACE THE WORD ARE

THE ARE ARE
ARE SAY YOU
ME ARE FOR

ARE

Draw a picture of the sentence

ARE YOU SAD?
ARE YOU
ARE

I

I LIKE TO PLAY.

I I I I

FIND AND TRACE THE WORD I

YOU I WE MY I
  I   SAY I
         THE

I

Draw a picture of the sentence

I AM HAPPY.

I AM

I

DO

I WILL DO MY BEST!

DO   DO   DO

FIND AND TRACE THE WORD DO

MY   DO   DO
I   YOU   DO
   DO   THE   THE

DO

Draw a picture of the sentence

I DO CHORES.

I DO

I DO

24

THE CAT WAS HAPPY.

WAS WAS WAS

FIND AND TRACE THE WORD **WAS**

WAS   DO   WAS
ME   WAS   YOU
   WAS   THE   LOOK

WAS

Draw a picture of the sentence

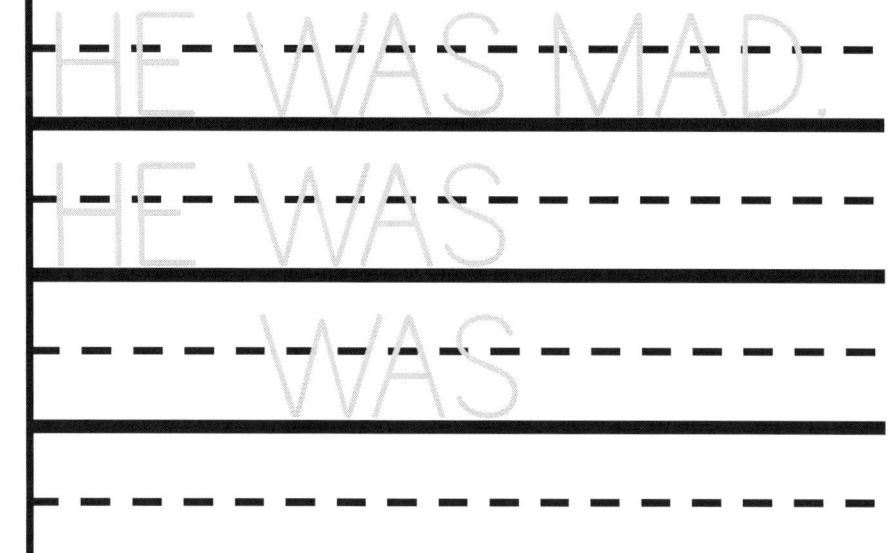

HE WAS MAD.

HE WAS

WAS

WE WILL HAVE FUN!

HAVE   HAVE

FIND AND TRACE THE WORD HAVE

HAVE   HAVE   HAVE
LOOK   THE   HAVE
   ME   ARE
                THE

HAVE

Draw a picture of the sentence

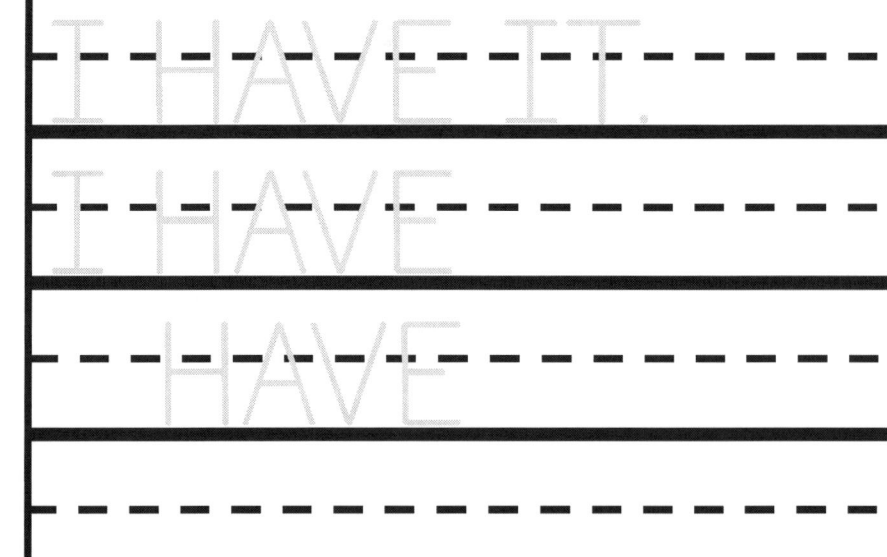

I HAVE IT.

I HAVE

HAVE

Tic-Tac-Toe Review

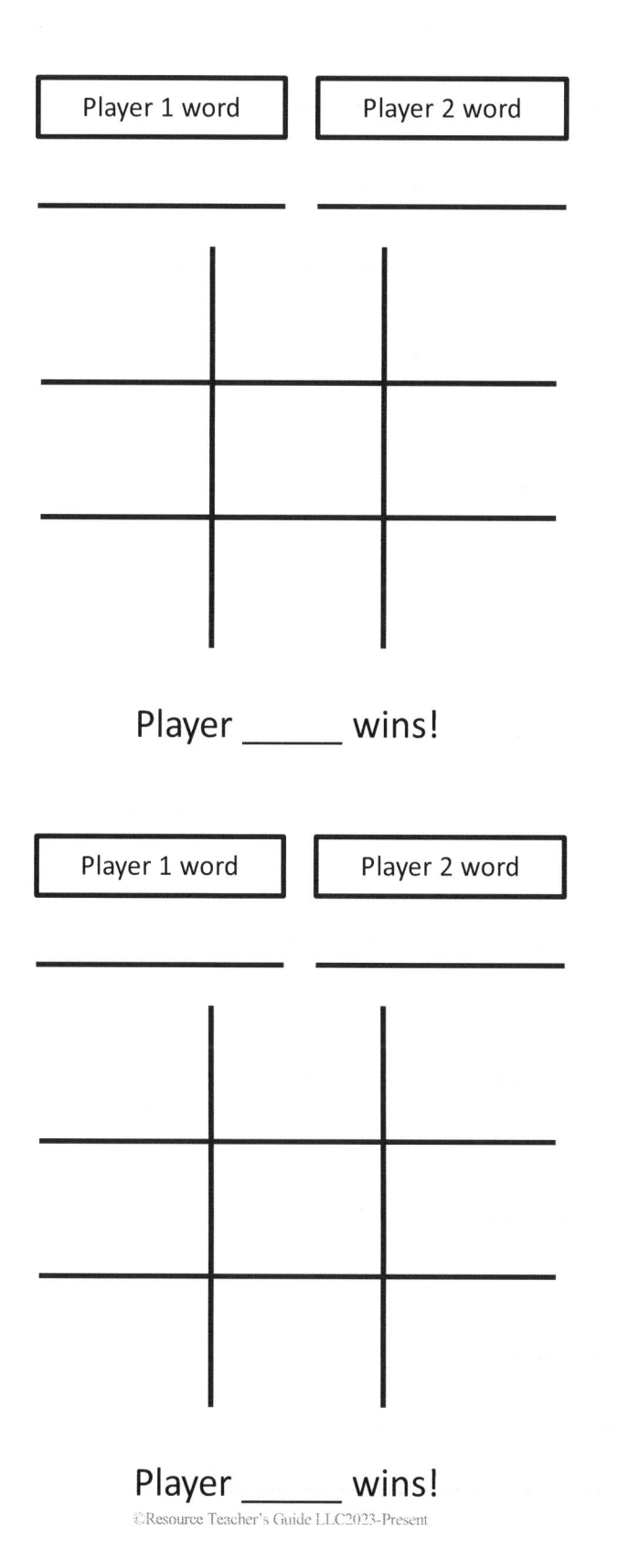

1. Each player picks a sight word and writes it on their line
2. Take turns writing your sight word in a spot on the tic-tac-toe
3. First to three in a row wins

| Player 1 word | Player 2 word |

Player _____ wins!

| Player 1 word | Player 2 word |

Player _____ wins!

| Player 1 word | Player 2 word |

Player _____ wins!

| Player 1 word | Player 2 word |

Player _____ wins!

©Resource Teacher's Guide LLC 2023-Present

WHAT IS THAT?

WHAT   WHAT

FIND AND TRACE THE WORD **WHAT**

WHAT

Draw a picture of the sentence

WHAT IS IT?
WHAT IS
WHAT

I LIKE IT HERE.

HERE HERE HERE

FIND AND TRACE THE WORD HERE

LOOK HERE DO
YOU SAY HERE
ME HERE
HERE

HERE

Draw a picture of the sentence

I AM HERE.
I _____ HERE.
_____ HERE.
_____

FIND

I WILL FIND THE LOST TOY.

FIND   FIND

FIND AND TRACE THE WORD FIND

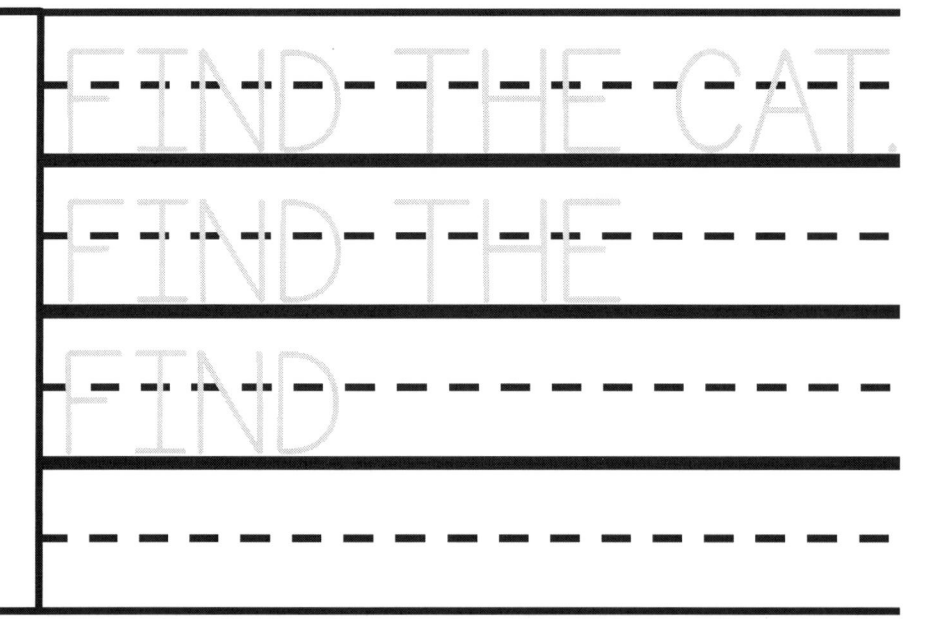

FIND   SAID   FIND
FIND   YOU
   ME   FIND   DO
                  THE

FIND

Draw a picture of the sentence

FIND THE CAT.
FIND THE
FIND

30

WHO ARE YOU?

WHO WHO

FIND AND TRACE THE WORD WHO

HERE WHO I
THE   SAY   YOU
    WHO FIND   WHO

WHO

Draw a picture of the sentence

WHO IS IT?
WHO IS
WHO

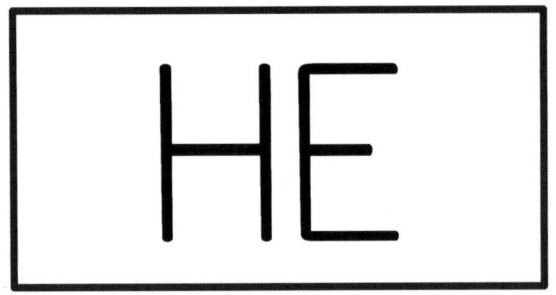

HE IS MY FRIEND!

HE HE HE HE

FIND AND TRACE THE WORD HE

HE   YOU   HE
FIND   SAY   WHO
     ME HE
              HE

HE

Draw a picture of the sentence

HE IS BIG!

HE IS

HE

SHE

SHE IS KIND.

SHE SHE SHE

FIND AND TRACE THE WORD SHE

HERE　SHE　　　THE
WHO　　　SO　　　SHE
　SHE　SHE　　HE

SHE

Draw a picture of the sentence

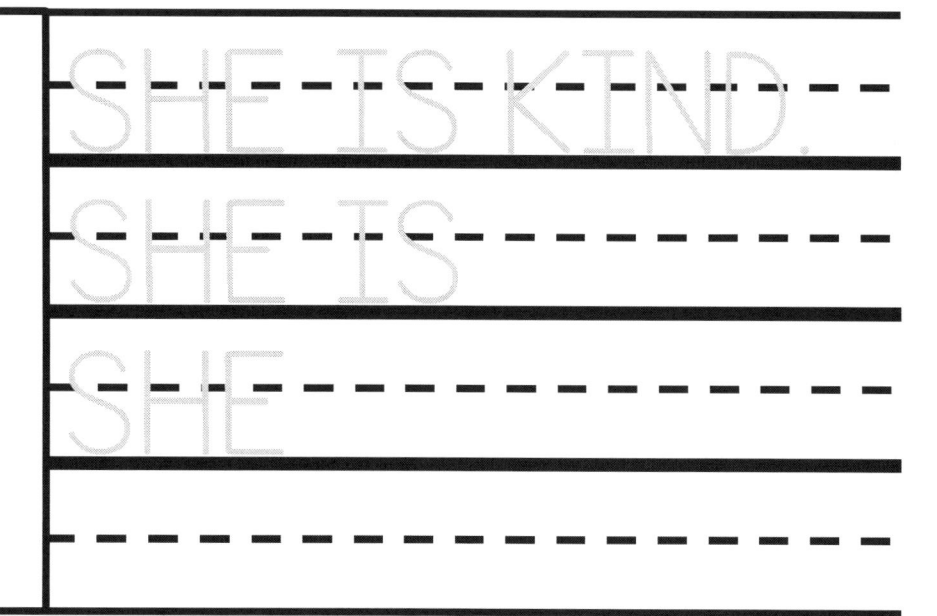

SHE IS KIND.
SHE IS
SHE

YOU SAW THE ICECREAM TRUCK!

SAW SAW SAW

FIND AND TRACE THE WORD SAW

SHE SAW SAW
SAW DO ARE
  WAS SAW HERE

SAW

Draw a picture of the sentence

I SAW A HOG.
I SAW
SAW

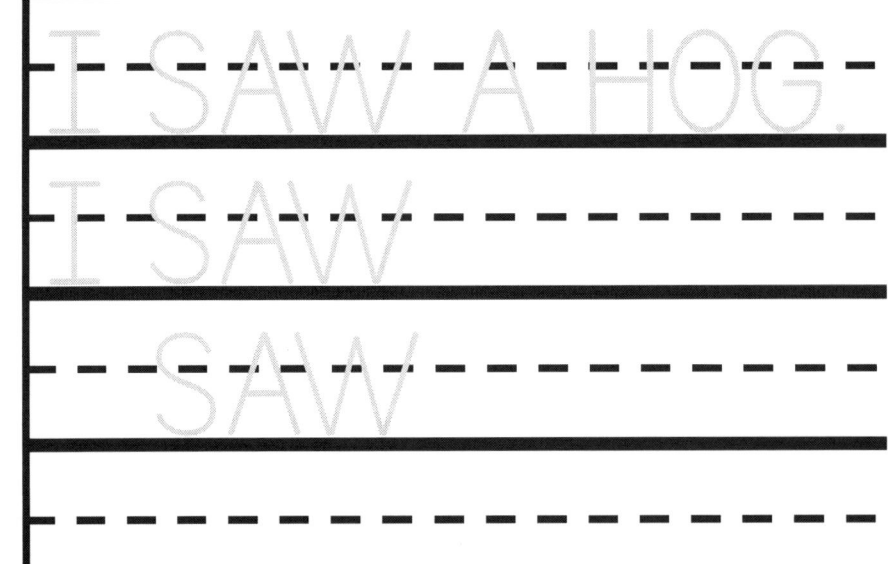

THEY ARE GRATEFUL FOR YOU!

THEY THEY

FIND AND TRACE THE WORD **THEY**

THEY WHO THEY
DO   WAS WHAT
THEY THEY COME

THEY

Draw a picture of the sentence

THEY CAN RUN.
THEY CAN
THEY

THERE IS GOOD IN EACH DAY.

THERE   THERE

FIND AND TRACE THE WORD **THERE**

FOR   THERE   FIND
THERE   WHO   THERE
HERE   GO   THERE

THERE

Draw a picture of the sentence

THERE IT IS!

THERE IT

THERE

©Resource Teacher's Guide LLC2023-Present

LITTLE

I AM A LITTLE BIT SCARED!

LITTLE LITTLE LITTLE

FIND AND TRACE THE WORD LITTLE

SAW LITTLE MY
WAS LITTLE LITTLE SEE
WHO LITTLE LITTLE

LITTLE

Draw a picture of the sentence

A LITTLE CAT
A LITTLE
LITTLE

Roll and Write

1. Pick 6 sight words, write one on each line on the bottom row above the dice
2. Roll a dice and find the number on your paper
3. Write the sight word in the column
4. Whichever sight word reaches the top first wins!

winner!	winner!	winner!	winner!	winner!	winner!

PLAY

I WILL PLAY WITH YOU!

PLAY PLAY PLAY

FIND AND TRACE THE WORD PLAY

LOOK YOU   PLAY
PLAY   PLAY SAID   PLAY
    THE   THERE

PLAY

Draw a picture of the sentence

PLAY WITH IT.
PLAY WITH
PLAY
- - -

A

HE IS A COOL FRIEND.

A A A A A

FIND AND TRACE THE WORD A

FIND A LITTLE
PLAY HAVE A THE
A A

A

Draw a picture of the sentence

A CAT NAPS.

A CAT

A

TOO

I WILL GO TOO!

TOO TOO TOO

FIND AND TRACE THE WORD TOO

LITTLE THERE TOO
TOO ME TOO
  TOO
HAVE LOOK

TOO

Draw a picture of the sentence

I ATE IT TOO.

I ATE TOO.

TOO.

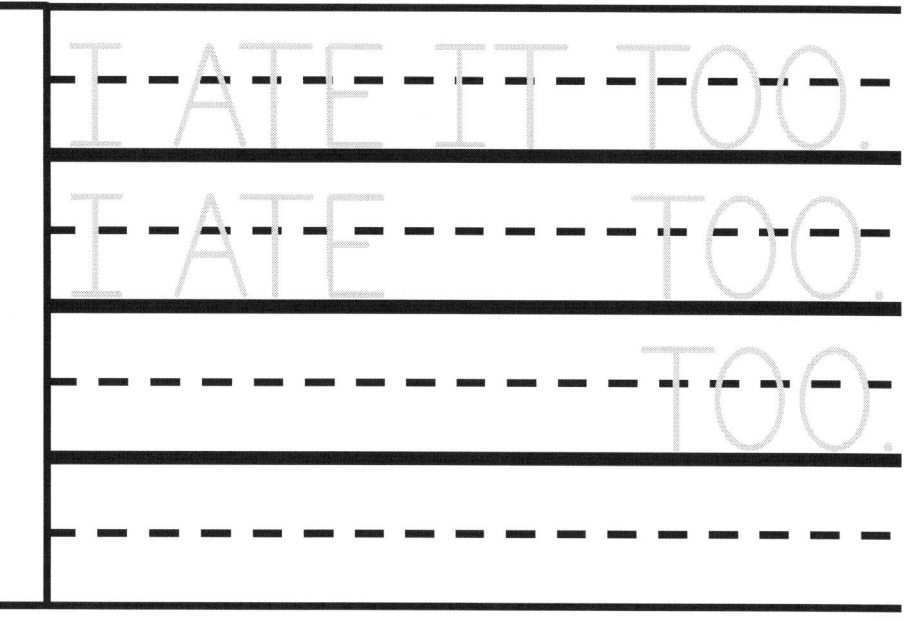

SO

THERE IS SO MUCH TO SEE!

SO   SO   SO   SO   SO

FIND AND TRACE THE WORD SO

SO   HERE   SO
WHAT   SO   SHE
        SO
WAS   HE

SO

DRAW A PICTURE OF THE SENTENCE

I'M SO TIRED.

I'M SO

SO

42

OUR

OUR FRIENDS WILL
BE SO GLAD.

OUR   OUR   OUR

FIND AND TRACE THE WORD OUR

OUR   I   OUR
DO   COME   LOOK
     OUR
OUR   LITTLE

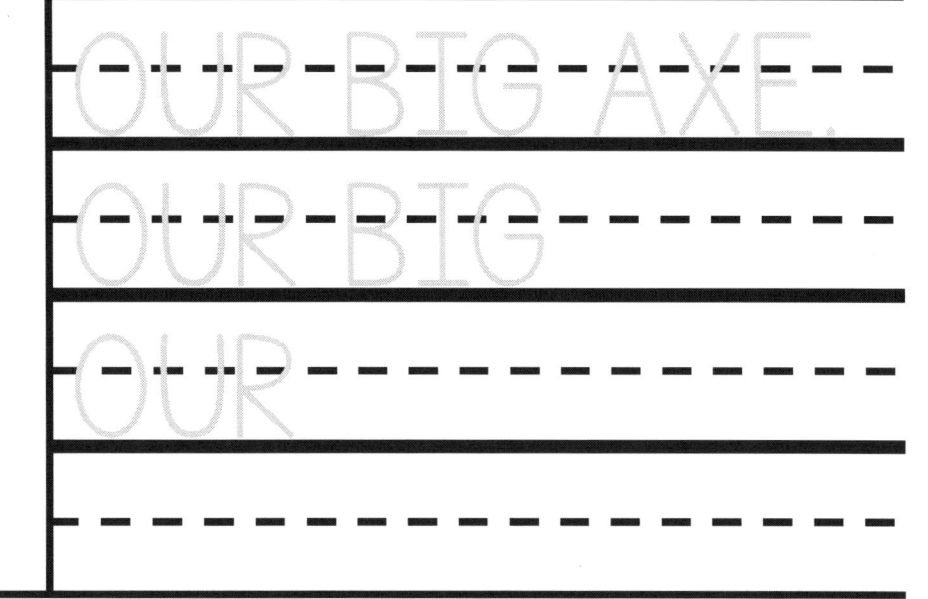

OUR

Draw a picture of the sentence

OUR BIG AXE.

OUR BIG

OUR

LIKE

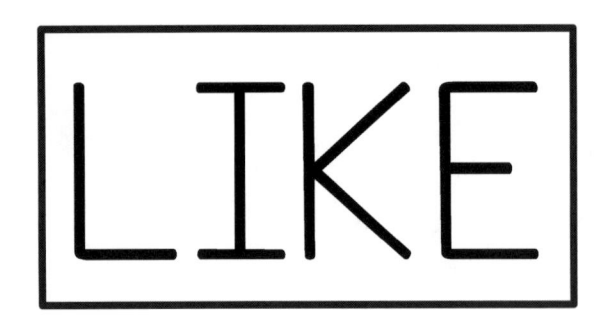

I LIKE TO DRAW PICTURES.

LIKE LIKE LIKE

FIND AND TRACE THE WORD LIKE

YOU LIKE MY
IS   LIKE   WE
SHE LIKE   LIKE

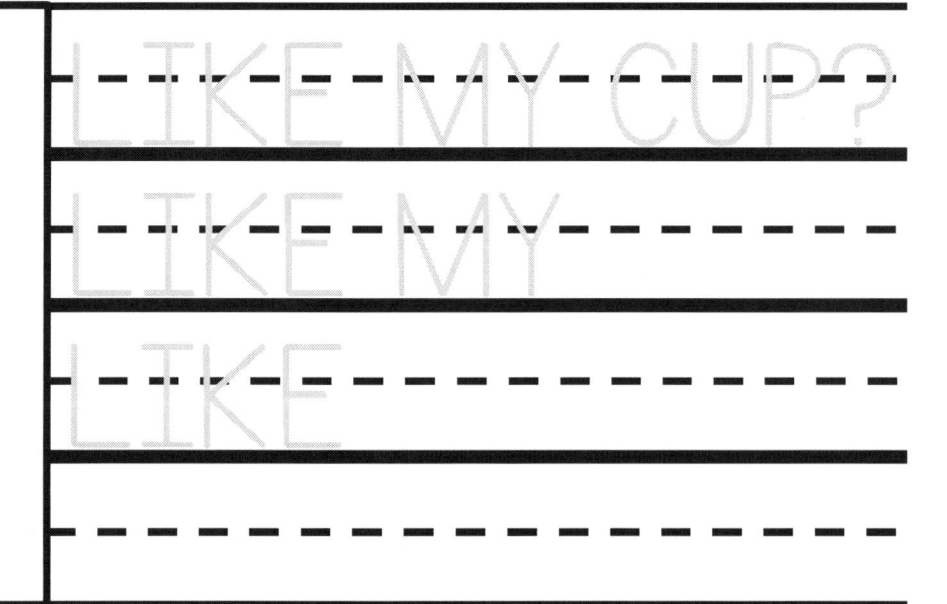

LIKE

Draw a picture of the sentence

LIKE MY CUP?
LIKE MY
LIKE

CAME

WE CAME IN FIRST.

CAME   CAME

FIND AND TRACE THE WORD CAME

TO   SEE   THE   CAME
  CAME CAME SHE   THE
              CAME

CAME

Draw a picture of the sentence

I CAME HOME.

I CAME

CAME

NOW

NOW WE CAN DO IT TOO.

NOW NOW NOW

FIND AND TRACE THE WORD NOW

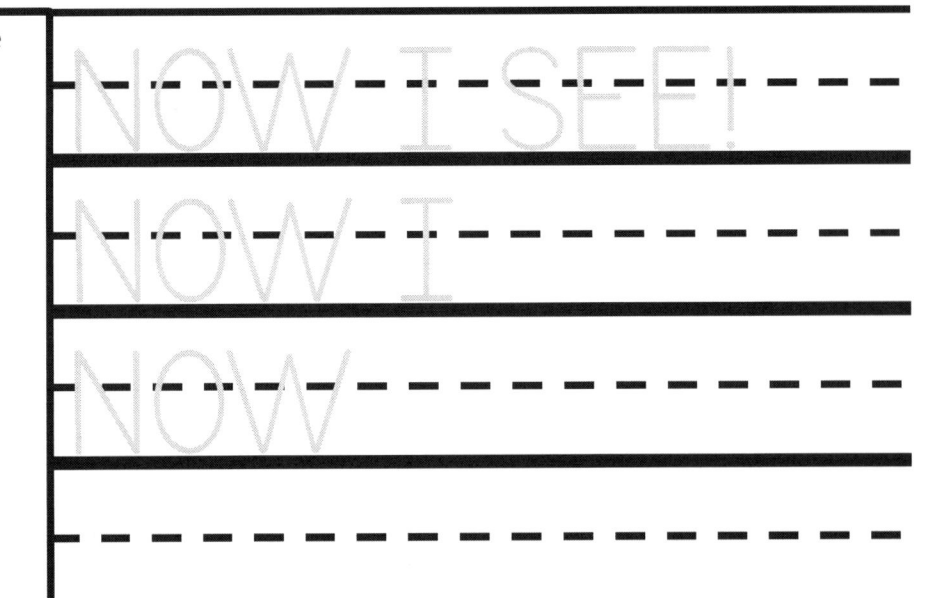

HAVE   NOW   NOW
WHO   NOW
         NOW   GO
WHAT   WHERE

NOW

Draw a picture of the sentence

NOW I SEE!
NOW I
NOW

ALL

I AM KEEPING IT ALL!

ALL ALL ALL

FIND AND TRACE THE WORD ALL

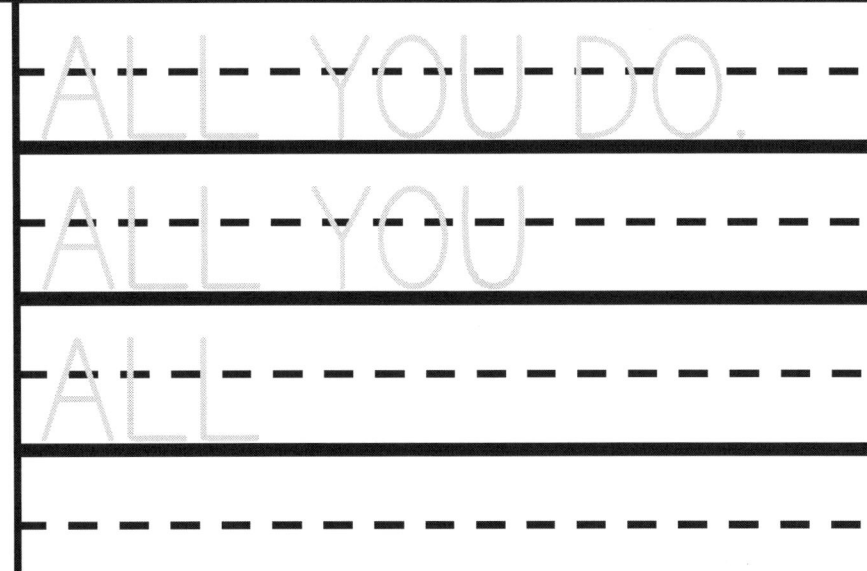

ARE ALL ALL
ALL WAS FIND
ALL HAVE
ALL HERE

ALL

Draw a picture of the sentence

ALL YOU DO.

ALL YOU

ALL

WANT

I WANT TO HANG OUT WITH YOU.

WANT   WANT

FIND AND TRACE THE WORD WANT

COME   WANT   LOOK
SAID   ME   WANT   I
WANT   WANT

WANT

Draw a picture of the sentence

WANT TO GO?

WANT TO

WANT

Tic-Tac-Toe Review

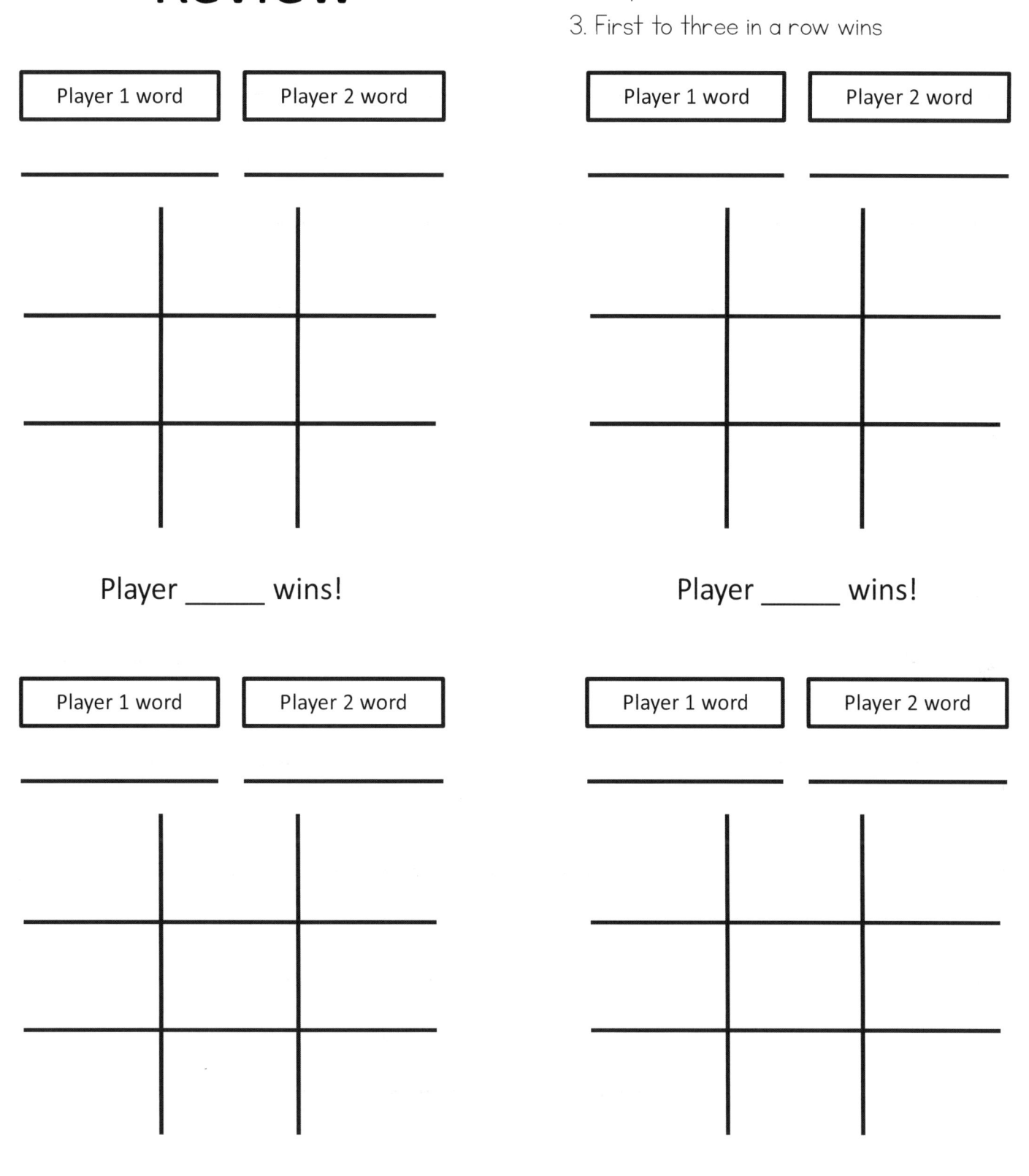

1. Each player picks a sight word and writes it on their line
2. Take turns writing your sight word in a spot on the tic-tac-toe
3. First to three in a row wins

| Player 1 word | Player 2 word |

Player _____ wins!

| Player 1 word | Player 2 word |

Player _____ wins!

| Player 1 word | Player 2 word |

Player _____ wins!

| Player 1 word | Player 2 word |

Player _____ wins!

NEW

I HAVE NEW SHOES.

NEW   NEW

FIND AND TRACE THE WORD NEW

TO   GO   WHERE

NEW   NEW   NEW   NEW
     SEE   AND

NEW

Draw a picture of the sentence

IT IS NEW.
IT IS NEW.
IT IS NEW.

AWAY

I MISS YOU WHEN YOU ARE AWAY.

AWAY   AWAY

FIND AND TRACE THE WORD AWAY

AWAY   SO   AWAY
WAS   MY   HE   LOOK
AWAY   AWAY

AWAY

Draw a picture of the sentence

SHE IS AWAY.
SHE _____ AWAY.
_____ _____ AWAY.

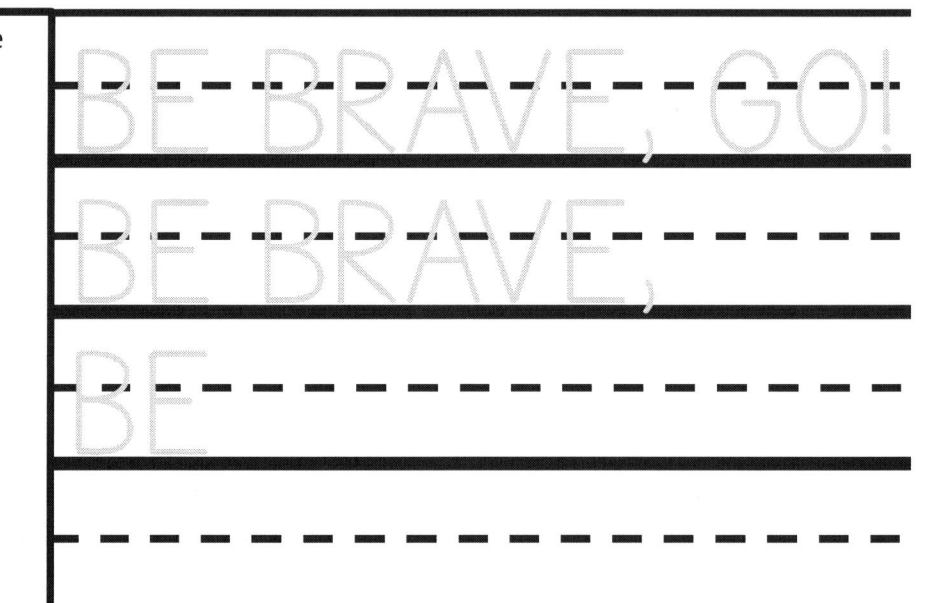

BE

LET'S BE FRIENDS FOREVER!

BE   BE   BE   BE

FIND AND TRACE THE WORD BE

ME   BE   BE
BE   BE   AND
      SAID
LOOK   COME

BE

Draw a picture of the sentence

BE BRAVE, GO!
BE BRAVE,
BE

NO

NO, I DON'T HAVE GUM.

NO NO NO NO

FIND AND TRACE THE WORD NO

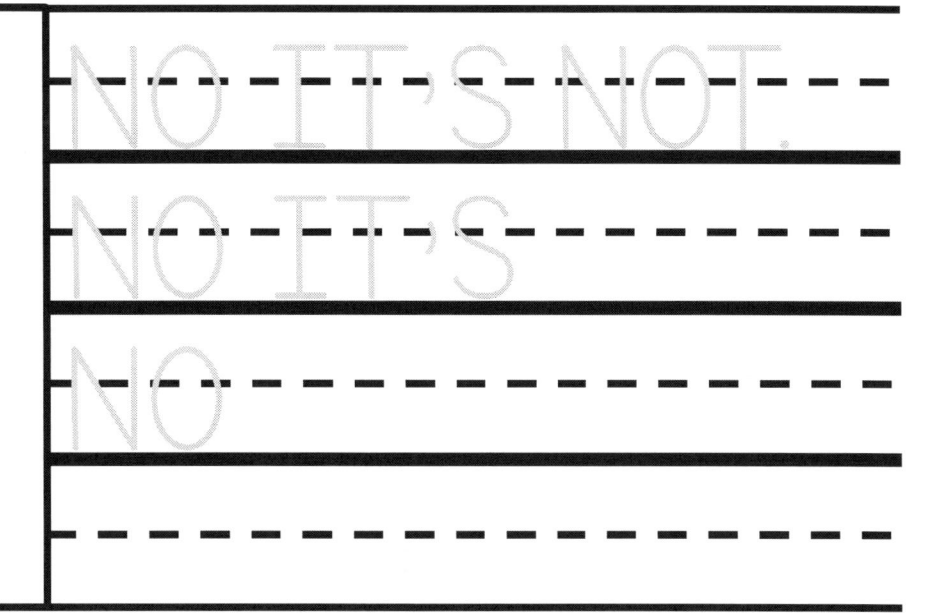

NO　　DO　　　　　ARE
HAVE　　　　I　　　NO
　　NO
WAS　　　　　NO

NO

Draw a picture of the sentence

NO IT'S NOT.

NO IT'S

NO

GOOD

WE ARE GOOD TO GO!

GOOD GOOD

FIND AND TRACE THE WORD GOOD

GOOD   GOOD   FIND
WHAT   GOOD   WHO
      HERE   HE
GOOD

GOOD

Draw a picture of the sentence

GOOD JOB!

GOOD JOB

GOOD

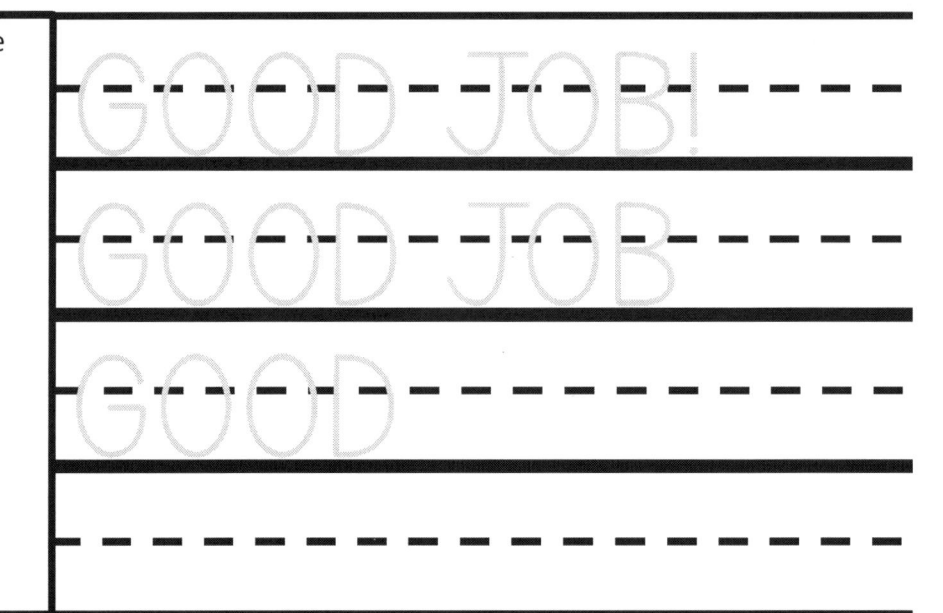

PUT

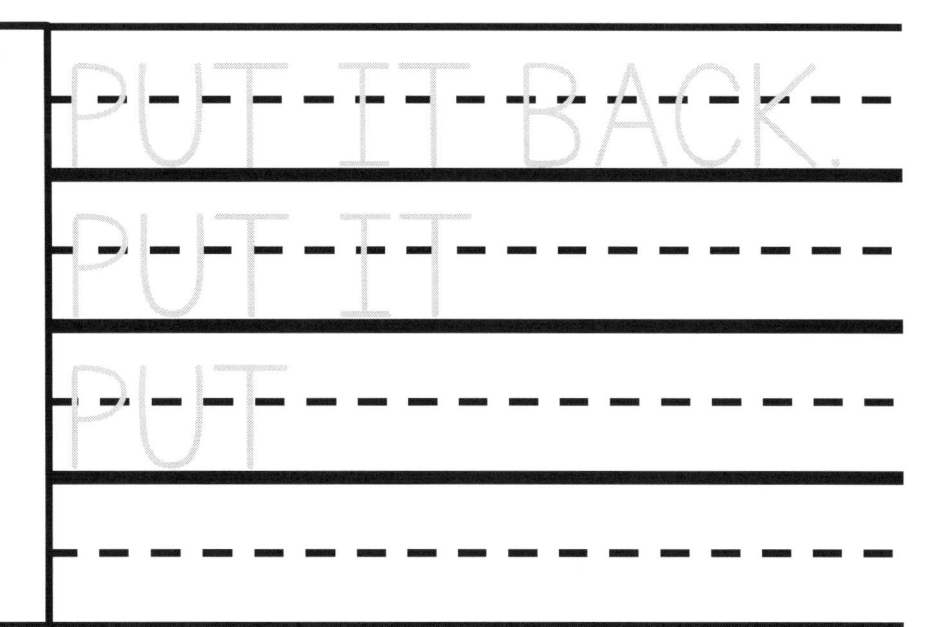

YOU CAN PUT THAT HERE.

PUT PUT PUT

FIND AND TRACE THE WORD PUT

AND PUT SHE
PUT COME HE
FOR PUT PUT

PUT

Draw a picture of the sentence

PUT IT BACK.

PUT IT

PUT

HER

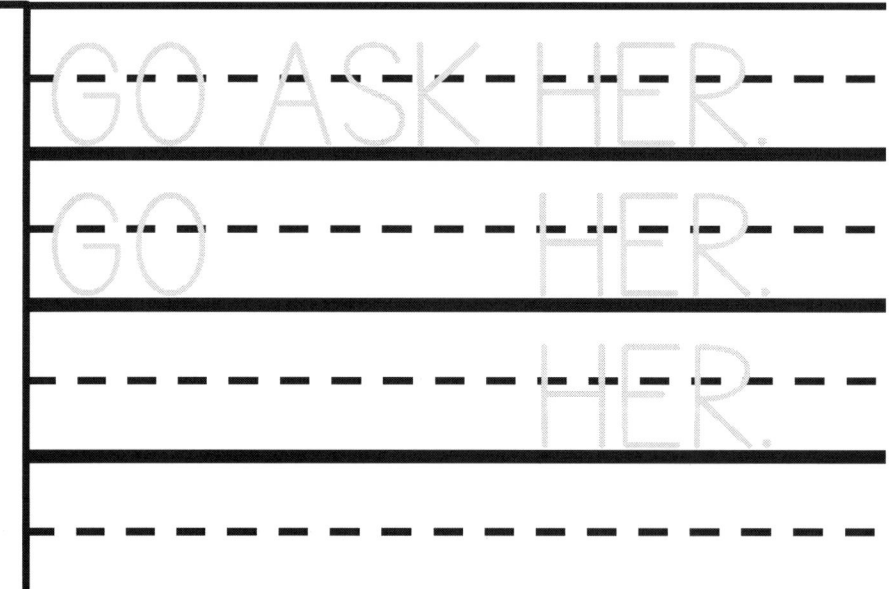

HER NOTEBOOK IS COOL.

HER   HER   HER

FIND AND TRACE THE WORD HER

PUT   CAME   HER
HER   LIKE   HER
     DO
   HER   NOW

HER

Draw a picture of the sentence

GO ASK HER.
GO ___ HER.
___ ___ HER.
___ ___ ___.

SOON

MY BIRTHDAY IS
SO SOON!

SOON   SOON

FIND AND TRACE THE WORD SOON

PLAY   SOON   THERE
SOON   SOON   SAW
LITTLE   SOON   SHE

SOON

Draw a picture of the sentence

IT IS SOON.

IT   SOON.

      SOON.

FROM

WHERE ARE YOU FROM?

FROM   FROM

FIND AND TRACE THE WORD FROM

FROM   WHO   FROM
WHAT   FIND   HE
            FROM
HERE   FROM

FROM

Draw a picture of the sentence

IT'S FROM ME!

IT'S FROM

FROM

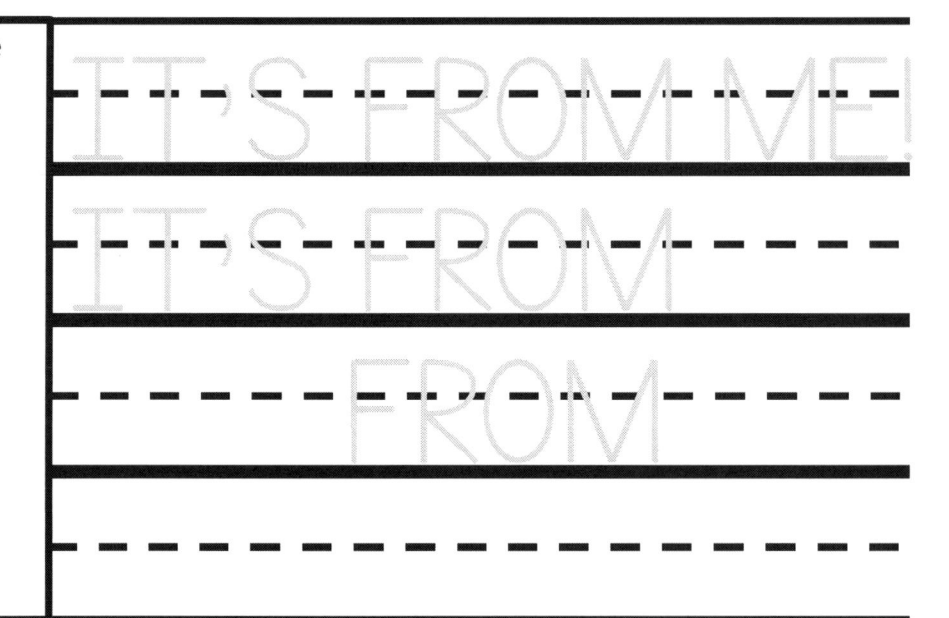

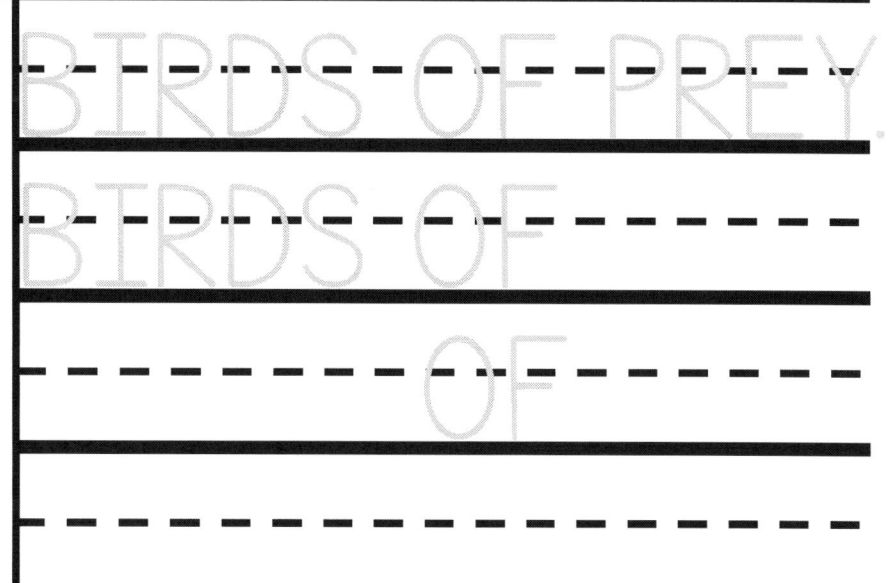

OF

I'M FULL OF CANDY.

OF OF OF

FIND AND TRACE THE WORD OF

OF HERE AND ME
        OF COME OF
    OF   OF   SAID

OF

Draw a picture of the sentence

BIRDS OF PREY.

BIRDS OF

OF

REVIEW: WORD SEARCH

COPY EACH WORD IN THE WORD SEARCH THEN CROSS IT OFF IN THE WORD BANK

WORD BANK:

THE	IS	AND	SAW	TOO
MY	SEE	SAID	THEY	SO
FOR	WHERE	ME	LITTLE	OUR
YOU	GO	LOOK	PLAY	LIKE

```
W  G  D  F  L  I  T  T  L  E
H  T  H  E  T  E  V  W  M  P
E  P  L  A  Y  U  S  E  E  O
R  C  S  I  T  O  O  X  Y  Q
E  H  R  S  A  W  L  O  O  K
I  S  O  Q  N  T  H  E  Y  R
J  F  O  R  L  M  S  A  I  D
B  K  L  I  K  E  V  U  O  S
G  O  W  Z  A  N  D  T  U  Z
M  Y  A  X  Y  Y  W  X  R  Z
```

BY

I'LL COME BY YOUR CLASS.

BY --- BY --- BY --- BY

FIND AND TRACE THE WORD BY

AND   BY   CAME
SAID   FOR   what
   BY   PUT   BY

BY _____

Draw a picture of the sentence

STAND BY ME.

STAND BY

BY

COULD

WE COULD GET A DOG?

COULD   COULD

FIND AND TRACE THE WORD COULD

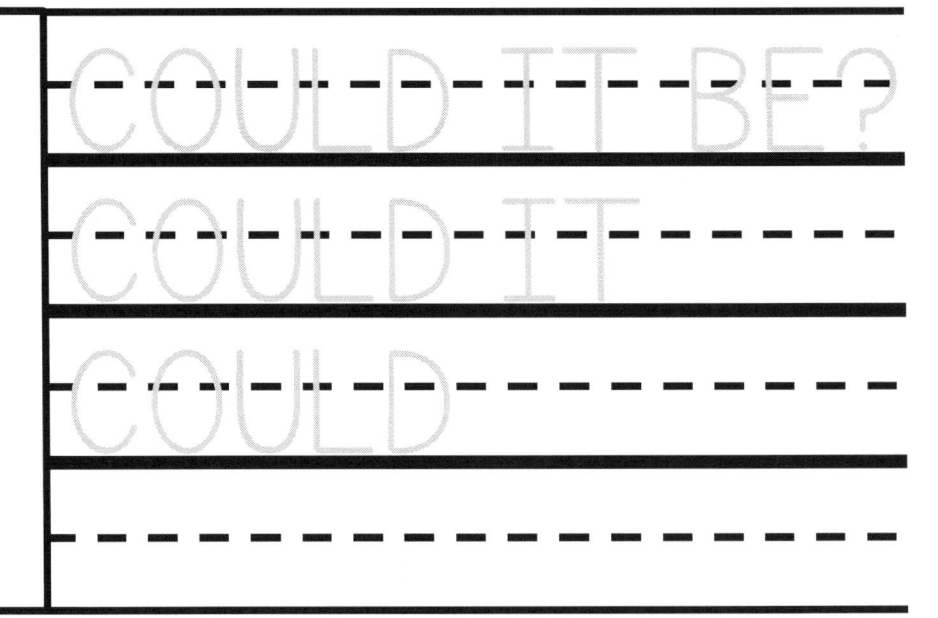

COULD   SOON   LIKE
WE   COULD   HAVE
       ARE   I
   COULD

COULD

Draw a picture of the sentence

COULD IT BE?

COULD IT

COULD

EVERY

I COUNTED EVERY CAR.

EVERY   EVERY

FIND AND TRACE THE WORD EVERY

PLAY   SOON   EVERY
EVERY   GO   SOON
LITTLE   EVERY
              EVERY

EVERY

Draw a picture of the sentence

EVERY ONE IS
EVERY ONE
EVERY

WHEN

WHEN WILL YOU EAT?

WHEN   WHEN

FIND AND TRACE THE WORD WHEN

WHEN   WHEN   COME
AND   SAID   WHEN
        LOOK
    WHEN   ME

WHEN

Draw a picture of the sentence

WHEN IS IT?

WHEN IS

WHEN

WERE

THEY WERE RUNNING FAST.

WERE   WERE

FIND AND TRACE THE WORD WERE

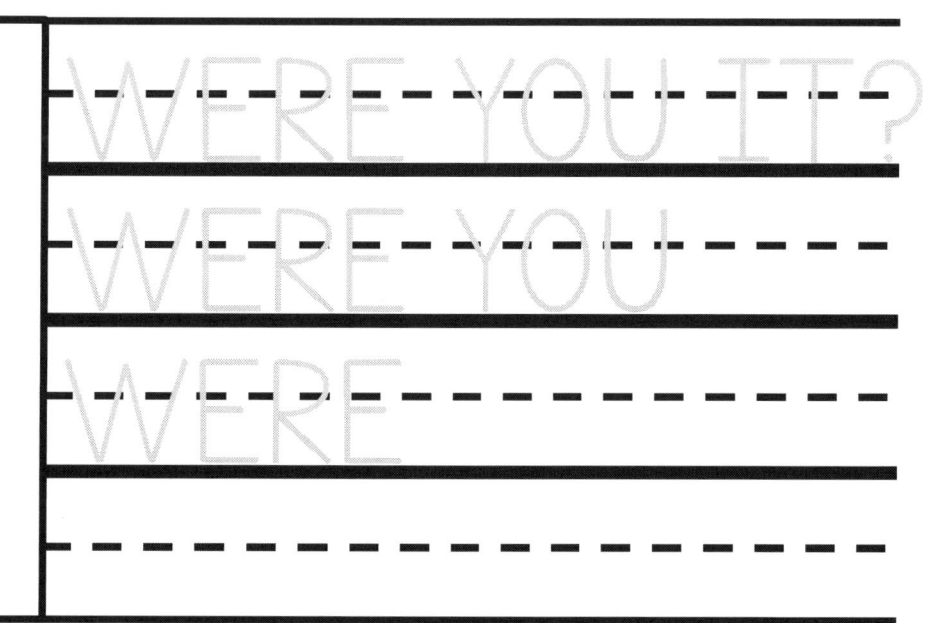

NOW   WERE   ALL
WERE   WERE   WANT
CAME   WERE   NEW

WERE

Draw a picture of the sentence

WERE YOU IT?

WERE YOU

WERE

GOING

WE ARE GOING TO DRAW.

GOING   GOING

FIND AND TRACE THE WORD GOING

THE   GOING   GOING
WE   GOING   WHAT
   GOING THEN GOING BY

GOING

Draw a picture of the sentence

GOING NOW?
GOING NOW
GOING

THEN

FIRST WE SWIM, THEN WE EAT!

THEN   THEN

FIND AND TRACE THE WORD THEN

THEN	MY	WE
FOR	THEN	THE
YOU	THEN	THEN

THEN

Draw a picture of the sentence

THEN WE CAN.

THEN WE

THEN

HAS

SHE HAS BEEN HAPPY YOU CAME!

HAS HAS HAS

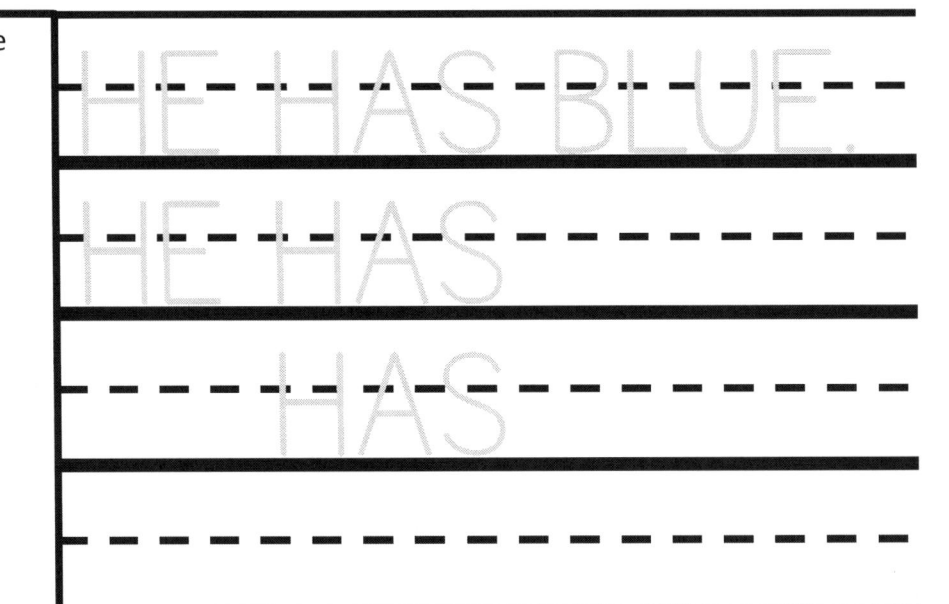

FIND AND TRACE THE WORD HAS

HAS   HAS   TO
GO   WHERE   SEE
HAS   HAS
                IS

HAS

Draw a picture of the sentence

HE HAS BLUE.

HE HAS

HAS

HIS

HIS ICE CREAM IS MELTING.

HIS   HIS   HIS

FIND AND TRACE THE WORD HIS

COME   SAID   ME
AND   HIS   HIS
      HIS
HIS   LOOK

HIS

Draw a picture of the sentence

HIS TEAM IS.

HIS TEAM

HIS

JUST

I JUST WANT TO PLAY!

JUST   JUST

FIND AND TRACE THE WORD JUST

JUST   DO   JUST
ARE   I   HAVE
       WAS
JUST   JUST

JUST

Draw a picture of the sentence

JUST GET UP.

JUST GET

JUST

Roll and Write

1. Pick 6 sight words, write one on each line on the bottom row above the dice
2. Roll a dice and find the number on your paper
3. Write the sight word in the column
4. Whichever sight word reaches the top first wins!

winner!	winner!	winner!	winner!	winner!	winner!

KNOW

I KNOW HOW TO DO THAT.

KNOW   KNOW

FIND AND TRACE THE WORD KNOW

HAVE   LIKE   KNOW
KNOW   GO   NOW
   KNOW
WHAT   KNOW

KNOW

Draw a picture of the sentence

I KNOW YOU!

I KNOW

KNOW

UNDER

I WALK UNDER
THE BRIDGE.

UNDER   UNDER

FIND AND TRACE THE WORD UNDER

UNDER   UNDER   WHERE
WHO   KNOW   NOW
   WHAT   UNDER
                   UNDER

UNDER

Draw a picture of the sentence

LOOK THERE.

LOOK THERE

LOOK

AGAIN

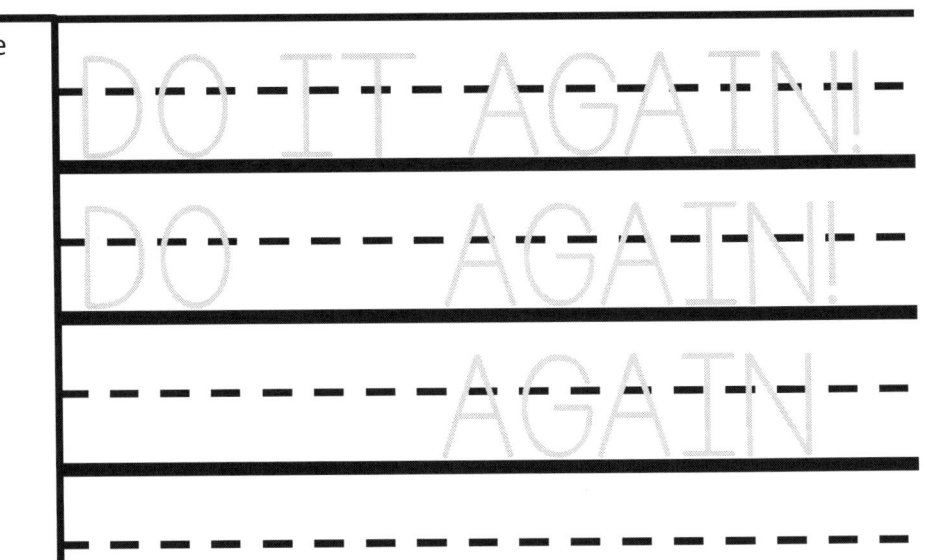

HE CAN PLAY THAT AGAIN.

AGAIN   AGAIN

FIND AND TRACE THE WORD AGAIN

AGAIN   WE   AGAIN
WHO   I   NOW
    AGAIN   AGAIN   WHERE

AGAIN

Draw a picture of the sentence

DO IT AGAIN!
DO   AGAIN!
AGAIN

ONCE

ONCE UPON A TIME.

ONCE ONCE

FIND AND TRACE THE WORD ONCE

HAVE ONCE ONCE
ONCE   GO   WE
     NOW
ONCE   WHERE

ONCE

Draw a picture of the sentence

SAY IT ONCE.
SAY ONCE.
ONCE.

FUNNY

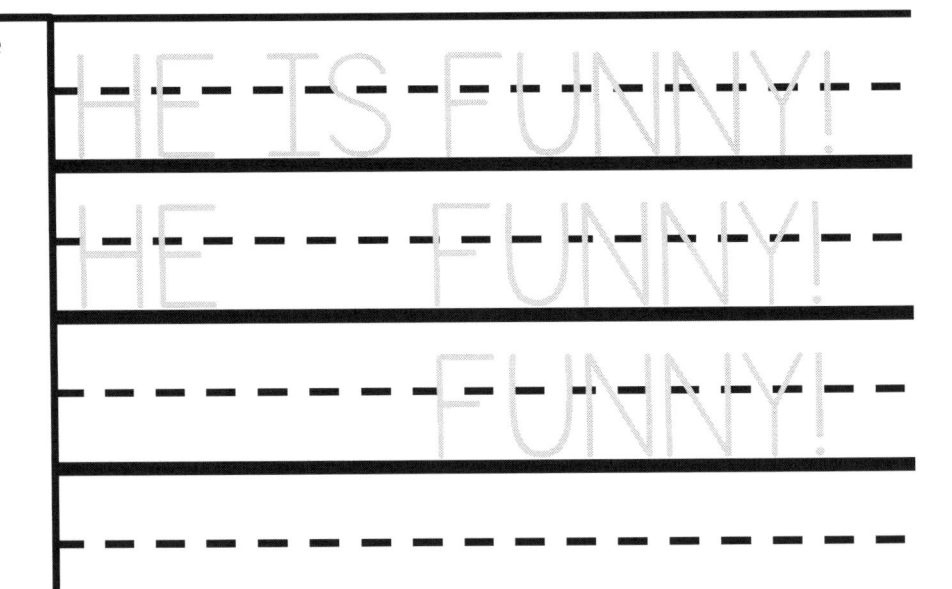

THAT WAS FUNNY!

FUNNY   FUNNY

FIND AND TRACE THE WORD FUNNY

HAVE   NOW   FUNNY
FUNNY   FUNNY   THE
   WHAT FIND   FUNNY

FUNNY

Draw a picture of the sentence

HE IS FUNNY!

HE   FUNNY!

FUNNY!

SOME

SOME PEOPLE LIKE SNOW.

SOME   SOME

FIND AND TRACE THE WORD SOME

SOME   ME   HAVE
HERE   WAS   SOME   SOME
    SOME   THE

SOME

Draw a picture of the sentence

SOME DO IT.

SOME DO

SOME

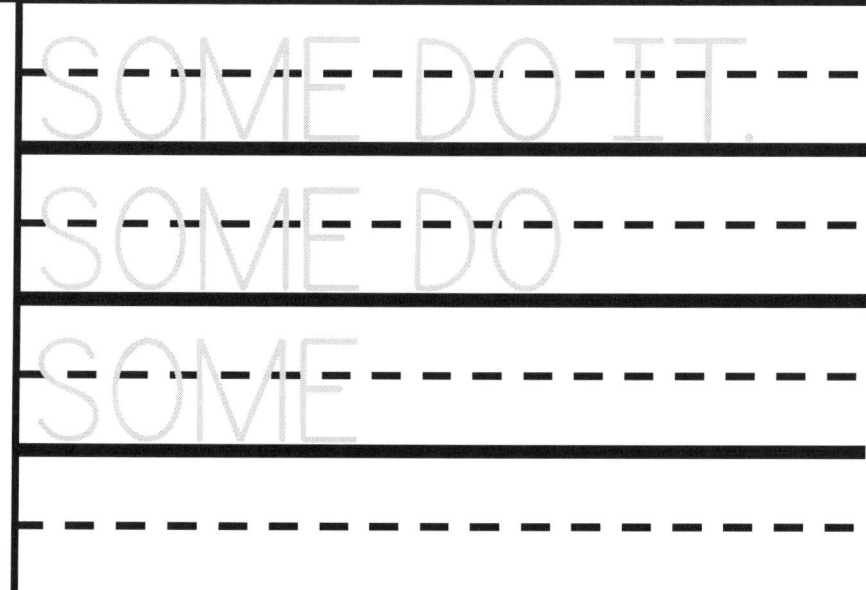

TAKE

HE WILL TAKE IT.

TAKE   TAKE

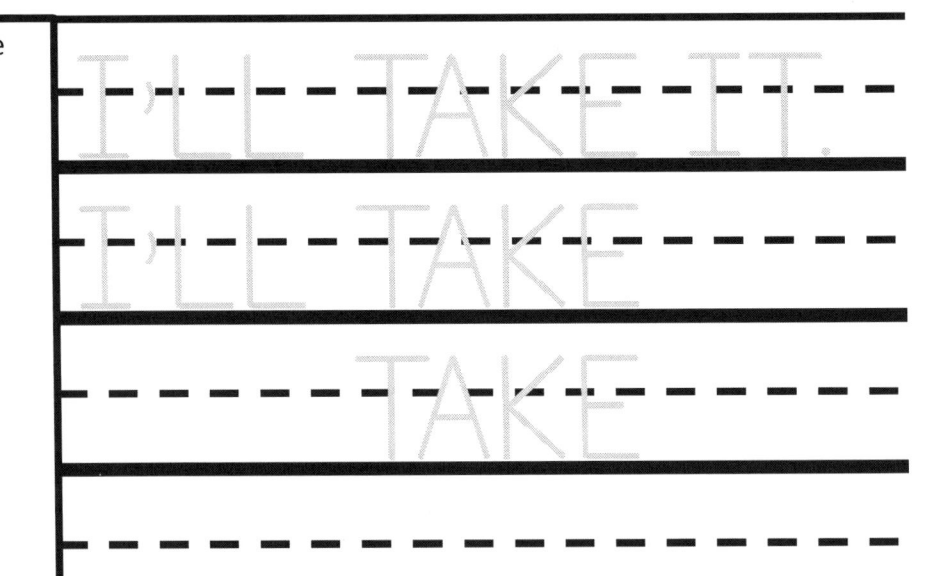

FIND AND TRACE THE WORD TAKE

TAKE	OF		THE
YOU		TAKE	ME
	ARE TAKE		TAKE

TAKE

Draw a picture of the sentence

I'LL TAKE IT.

I'LL TAKE

TAKE

THEM

BE KIND TO THEM.

THEM   THEM

FIND AND TRACE THE WORD THEM

THEM   OF   SHE
THEM   ARE   YOU
HERE SAY   THEM

THEM

Draw a picture of the sentence

I HAVE THEM.

I ___ THEM.

___ THEM.

PLEASE

HELP ME PLEASE!

PLEASE PLEASE

FIND AND TRACE THE WORD PLEASE

TAKE PLEASE PLEASE

YOU PLEASE SAY THEM

ME PLEASE

PLEASE

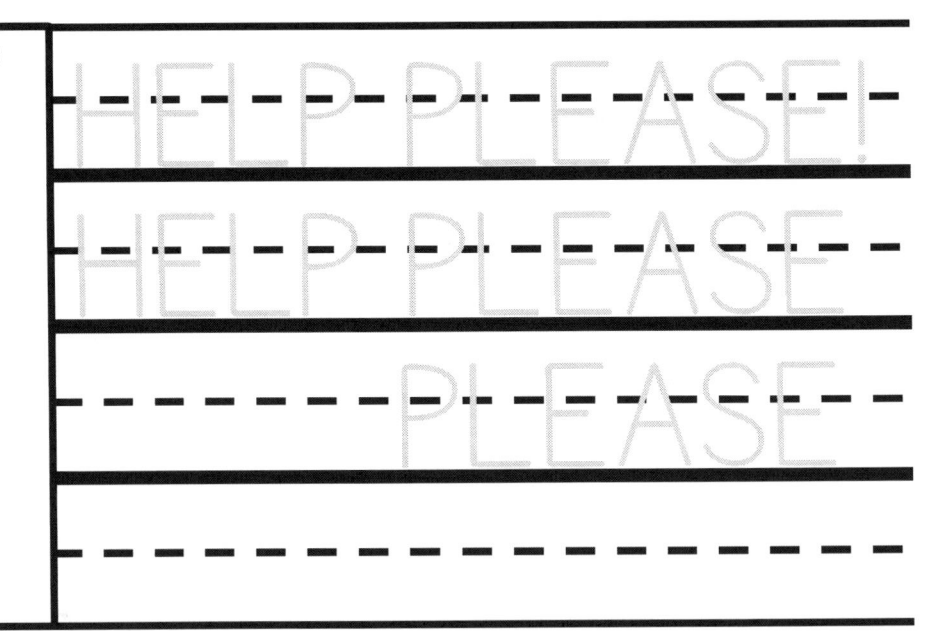

Draw a picture of the sentence

HELP PLEASE!

HELP PLEASE

PLEASE

AT

SHE IS GOOD AT THAT.

AT AT AT AT

FIND AND TRACE THE WORD AT

PLEASE OF AT
AT   AT   AT   ME
       ARE   SOME

AT

Draw a picture of the sentence

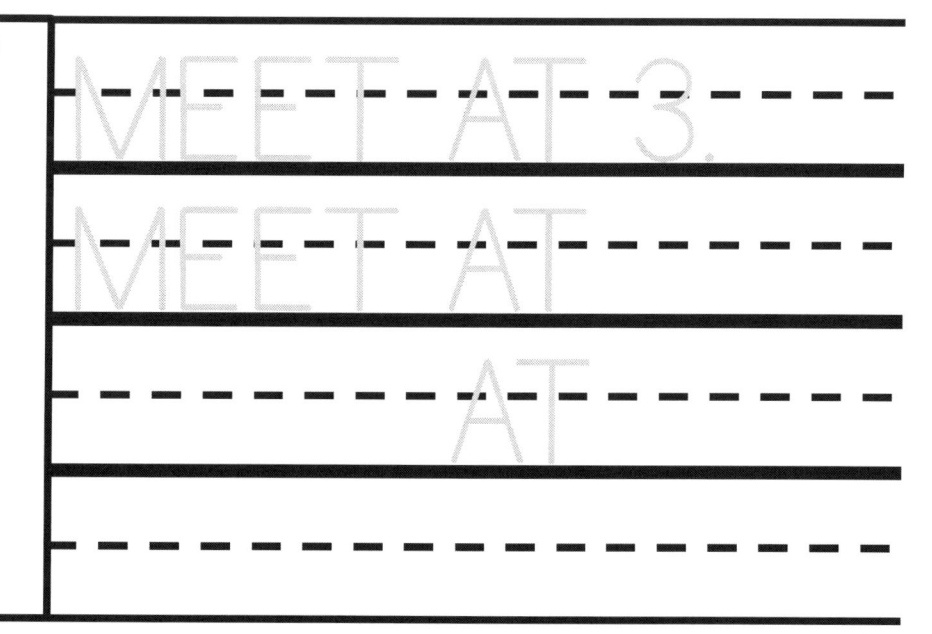

MEET AT 3.
MEET AT
AT

Tic-Tac-Toe Review

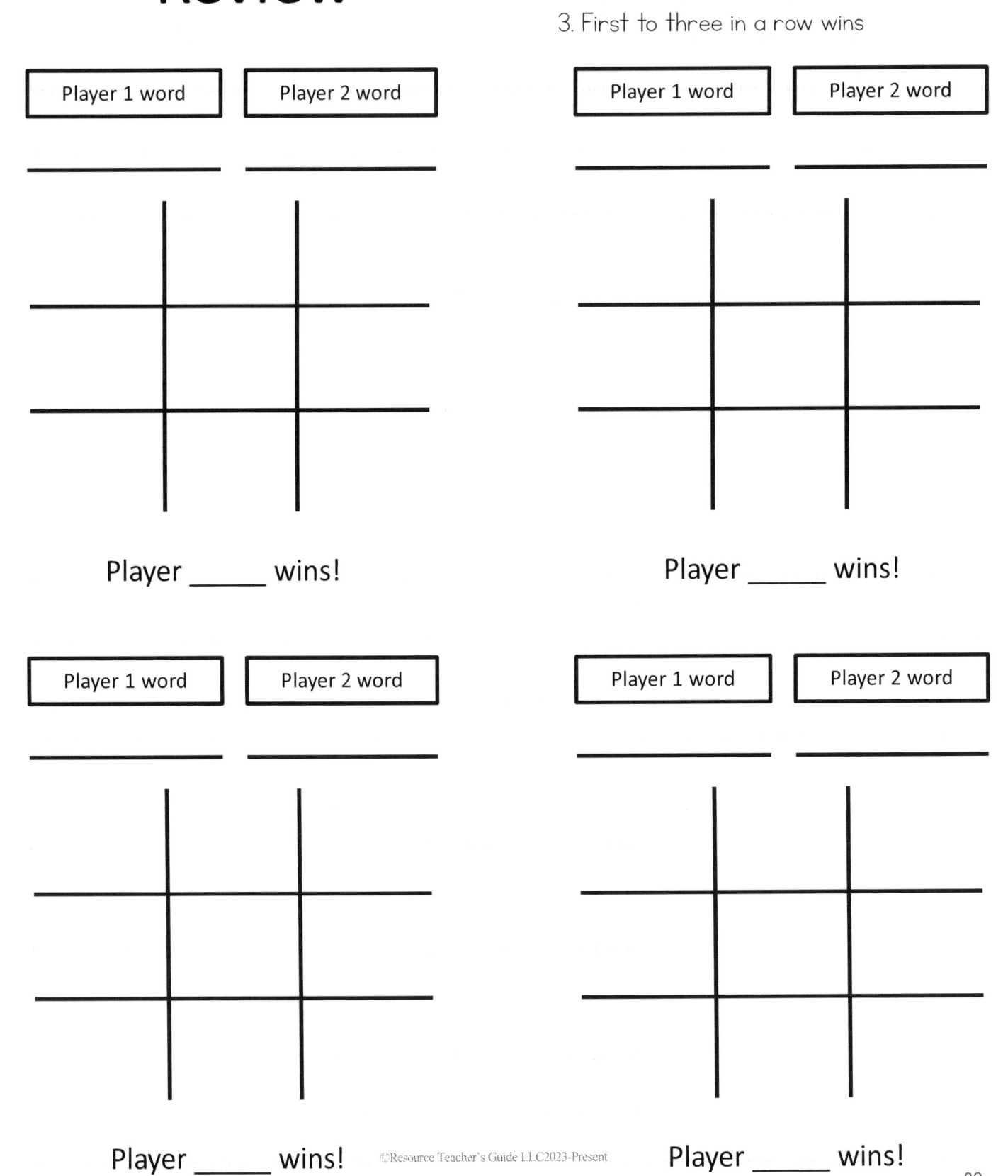

1. Each player picks a sight word and writes it on their line
2. Take turns writing your sight word in a spot on the tic-tac-toe
3. First to three in a row wins

| Player 1 word | Player 2 word |

Player _____ wins!

| Player 1 word | Player 2 word |

Player _____ wins!

| Player 1 word | Player 2 word |

Player _____ wins!

| Player 1 word | Player 2 word |

Player _____ wins!

YOUR

IS THAT YOUR WORK?

YOUR   YOUR

FIND AND TRACE THE WORD YOUR

WHO   YOUR   YOUR
FINE   HERE   YOUR
HE   YOUR
                  WHAT

YOUR

Draw a picture of the sentence

YOUR COAT!
YOUR COAT
YOUR

THAT

THAT WOULD BE SO HELPFUL.

THAT   THAT

FIND AND TRACE THE WORD THAT

SHE	THAT		THEY
THAT		SAW	THERE
	THAT		
THAT	THAT		LITTLE

THAT

Draw a picture of the sentence

THAT IS NICE.

THAT IS

THAT

OR

CHOCOLATE OR VANILLA?

OR OR OR OR

FIND AND TRACE THE WORD OR

A   OR   OR
TOO   OR   PLAY
        OUR
  SO   OR

OR

Draw a picture of the sentence

DAY OR NIGHT?
DAY OR
        OR

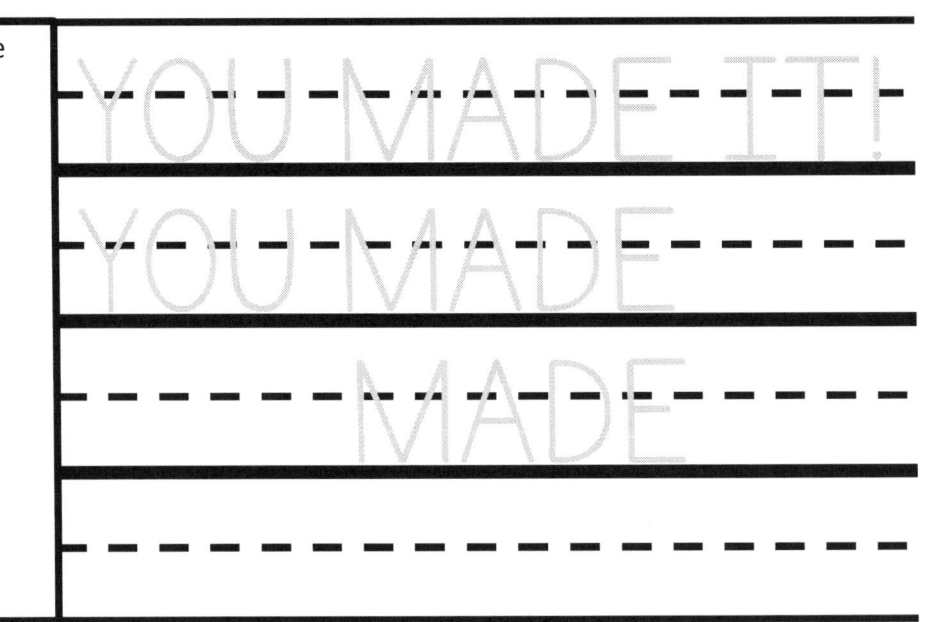

MADE

I MADE THIS
JUST FOR YOU.

MADE   MADE

FIND AND TRACE THE WORD MADE

MADE   MADE   NOW
LIKE   CAME   ALL
       MADE
   MADE   WANT

MADE

Draw a picture of the sentence

YOU MADE IT!

YOU MADE

MADE

IF

IF YOU ARE SAD
I CAN HELP.

IF IF IF IF IF

FIND AND TRACE THE WORD IF

IF   BE   NO
NEW   IF   if
   IF AWAY   GOOD

IF

Draw a picture of the sentence

IF IT RAINS.

IF IT

IF

GET

I GET TO SIT BY YOU!

GET GET GET

FIND AND TRACE THE WORD GET

PUT GET   GET
GET   SOON FROM
     GET HER
              OF

GET

Draw a picture of the sentence

I GET IT.

I GET

GET

HAD

I WISH WE HAD ALL DAY.

HAD   HAD   HAD

FIND AND TRACE THE WORD HAD

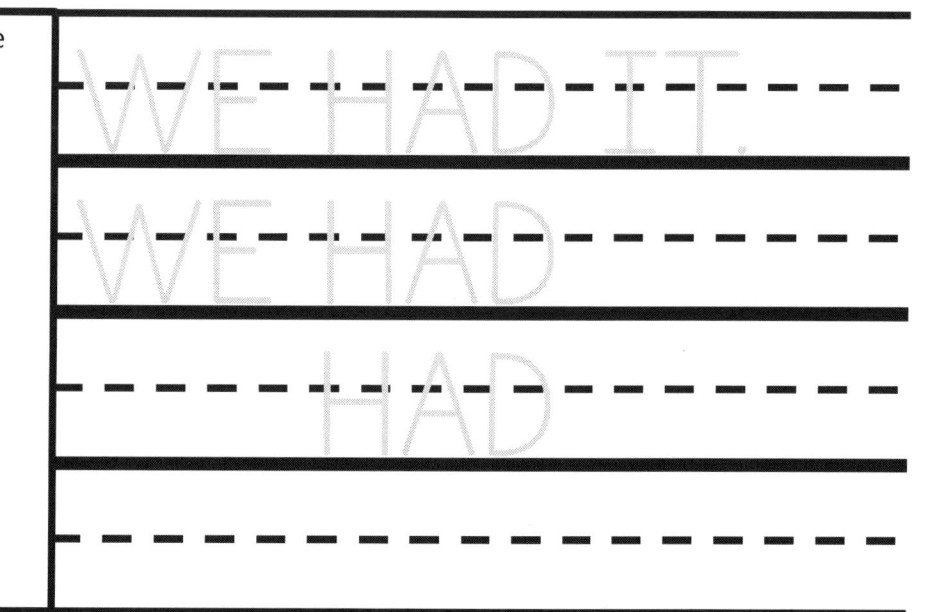

WHEN HAD BY
WERE COULD HAD
    HAD
EVERY HAD

HAD

Draw a picture of the sentence

WE HAD IT.

WE HAD

HAD

AS

YOU ARE AS BRIGHT AS THE SUN!

AS AS AS AS AS

FIND AND TRACE THE WORD AS

GOING AS AS
THEN HAS HIS
  AS
AS JUST

AS

Draw a picture of the sentence

GOOD AS ME.
GOOD AS
AS

DID

YOU DID IT!

DID   DID   DID

FIND AND TRACE THE WORD DID

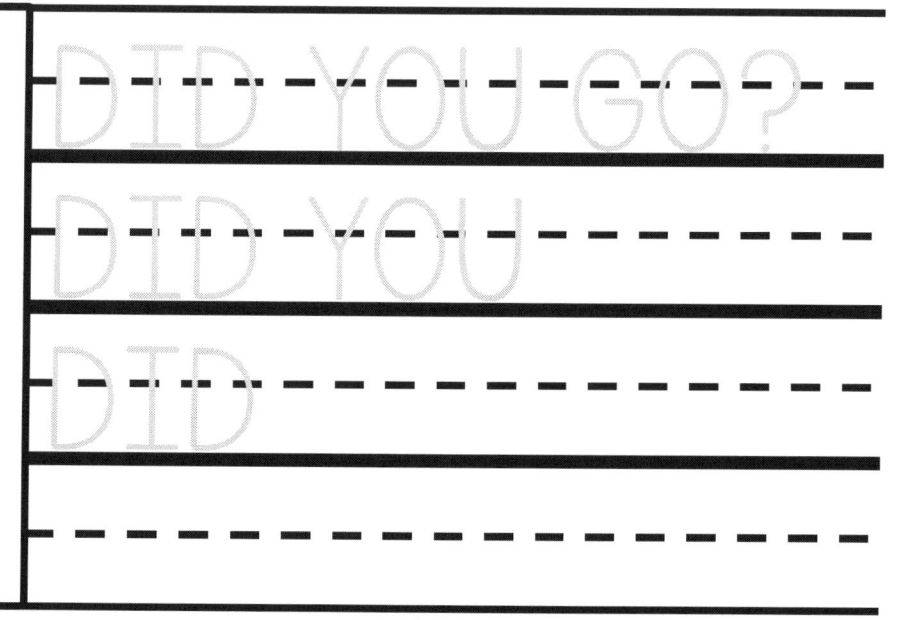

AGAIN   UNDER   DID
ONCE   DID   KNOW
    FUNNY   DID
            DID

DID

Draw a picture of the sentence

DID YOU GO?

DID YOU

DID

HOW

HOW ARE YOU FEELING?

HOW   HOW

FIND AND TRACE THE WORD HOW

HOW   PLEASE   TAKE
HOW   HOW   HOW
   AT   THEM   SOME

HOW

Draw a picture of the sentence

HOW IS IT?
HOW IS
HOW

Roll and Write

1. Pick 6 sight words, write one on each line on the bottom row above the dice
2. Roll a dice and find the number on your paper
3. Write the sight word in the column
4. Whichever sight word reaches the top first wins!

winner!	winner!	winner!	winner!	winner!	winner!
___	___	___	___	___	___
⚀	⚁	⚂	⚃	⚄	⚅

©Resource Teacher's Guide LLC 2023-Present

MAKE

MAKE ME SOME COOKIES PLEASE!

MAKE   MAKE

FIND AND TRACE THE WORD MAKE

THEM   MAKE   SOME
PLEASE   TAKE   AT
MAKE   MAKE   MAKE

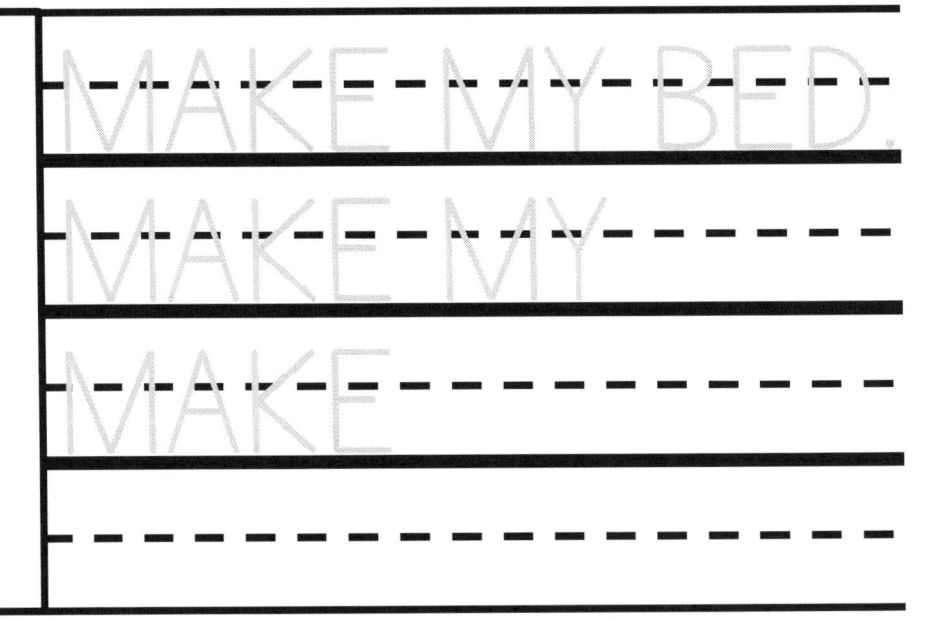

MAKE

Draw a picture of the sentence

MAKE MY BED.
MAKE MY
MAKE

IT

IT WOULD BE AMAZING!

IT IT IT

FIND AND TRACE THE WORD IT

YOUR   OR   IT
THAT   IT   IT
    IT MADE   IF

IT

Draw a picture of the sentence

IT IS GOOD!

IT IS

IT

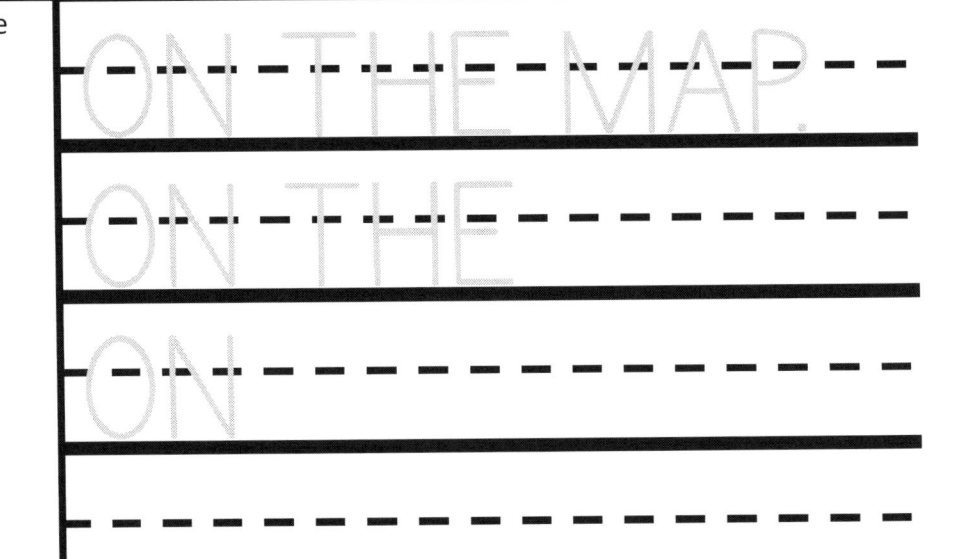

ON

YOU ARE ON AN AWESOME JOURNEY!

ON   ON   ON

FIND AND TRACE THE WORD ON

DID   ON   HAS
EVERY   ON   GET
HOW   ON
                ON

ON

Draw a picture of the sentence

ON THE MAP.
ON THE
ON

BUT

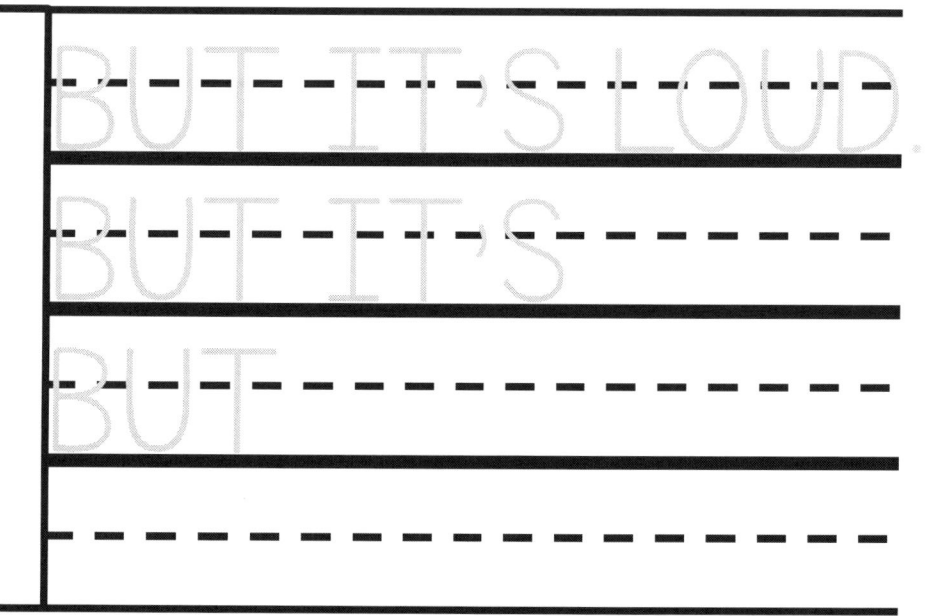

BUT CAN YOU GO WITH ME?

BUT   BUT   BUT

FIND AND TRACE THE WORD BUT

BUT   BUT   THE
BUT   YOU   WE
BUT   FOR   MY

BUT

Draw a picture of the sentence

BUT IT'S LOUD.
BUT IT'S
BUT

THIS

THIS GAME WENT FAST.

THIS   THIS

FIND AND TRACE THE WORD THIS

THIS   TOO   THIS
IS   THIS   WHERE
     SEE   GO
THIS

THIS

Draw a picture of the sentence

THIS IS FUN!

THIS IS

THIS

THAN

I'M SLEEPIER THAN A BABY.

THAN   THAN

FIND AND TRACE THE WORD THAN

SAID   LOOK   AND
THAN   COME   THAN
    ME   THAN
            THAN

THAN

Draw a picture of the sentence

RATHER THAN.
RATHER THAN
THAN

EACH

WE EACH GET HALF.

EACH   EACH

FIND AND TRACE THE WORD EACH

EACH   I   EACH
ARE   WAS   EACH
       DO
EACH   HAVE

EACH

Draw a picture of the sentence

EACH LID FIT.

EACH LID

EACH

OTHER

ALL THE OTHER KIDS
ARE GLAD TO SEE YOU.

OTHER   OTHER

FIND AND TRACE THE WORD OTHER

OTHER   OTHER   EVERY
EVERY   OTHER   SOON
LITTLE   OTHER   EVERY

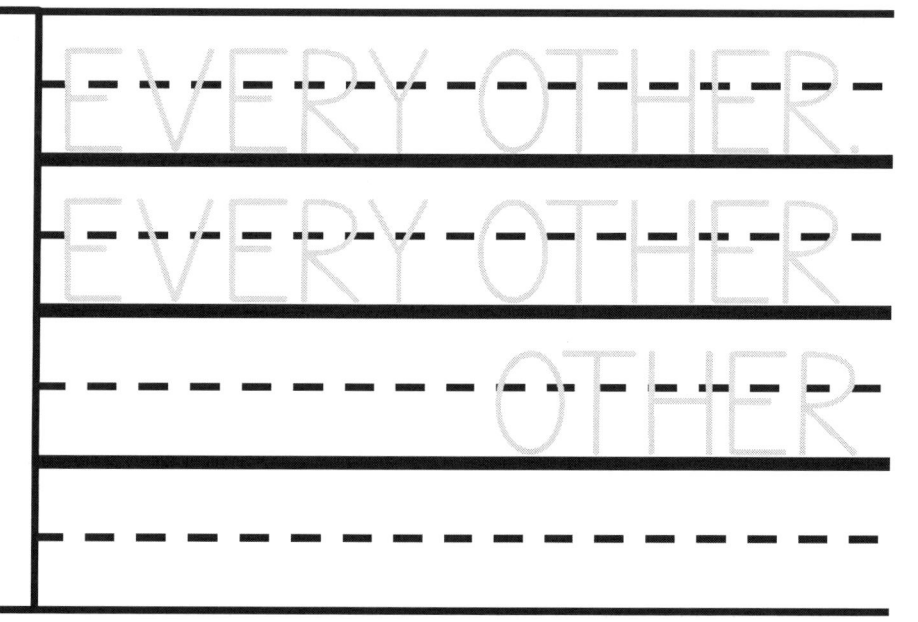

OTHER

Draw a picture of the sentence

EVERY OTHER.
EVERY OTHER
OTHER

WOULD

WOULD YOU LIKE TO JOIN US?

WOULD   WOULD

FIND AND TRACE THE WORD WOULD

HAVE   WOULD   I
WAS   ARE   DO
      WOULD
WOULD   WOULD

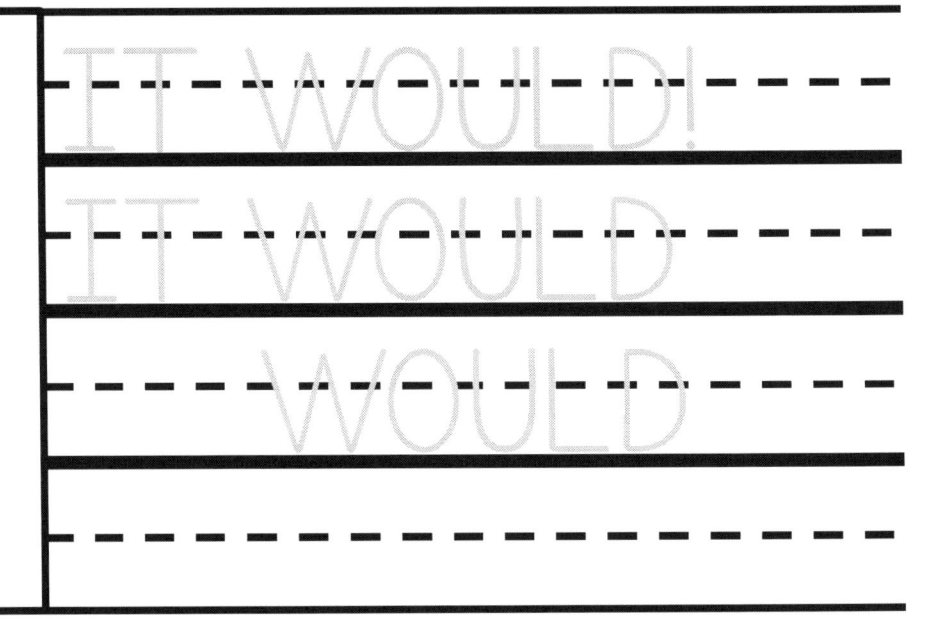

WOULD

Draw a picture of the sentence

IT WOULD!
IT WOULD
WOULD

NOT

THEY DID NOT GET DIRTY.

NOT NOT NOT

FIND AND TRACE THE WORD NOT

NOT HERE FIND
WHAT   NOT WHO
NOT NOT   HE

NOT

Draw a picture of the sentence

NOT IN HERE.

NOT IN

NOT

Tic-Tac-Toe Review

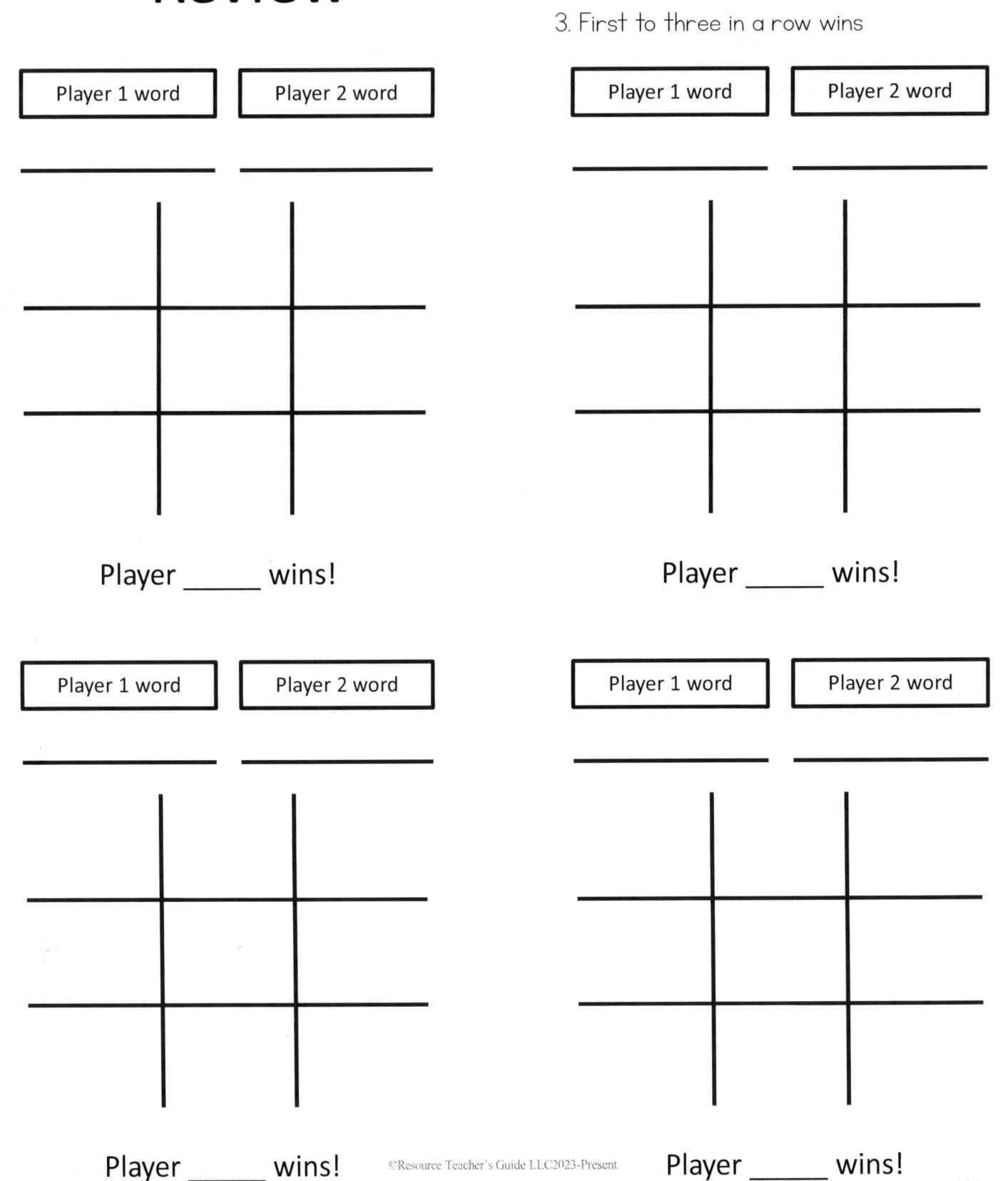

1. Each player picks a sight word and writes it on their line
2. Take turns writing your sight word in a spot on the tic-tac-toe
3. First to three in a row wins

| Player 1 word | Player 2 word |

Player _____ wins!

| Player 1 word | Player 2 word |

Player _____ wins!

| Player 1 word | Player 2 word |

Player _____ wins!

| Player 1 word | Player 2 word |

Player _____ wins!

ITS

ITS OWNER IS THE GIRL IN BLUE.

ITS ITS ITS

FIND AND TRACE THE WORD ITS

SAW ITS THERE
ITS THEY LOOK
SHE ITS ITS

ITS

Draw a picture of the sentence

ITS DOG BONE.
ITS DOG
ITS

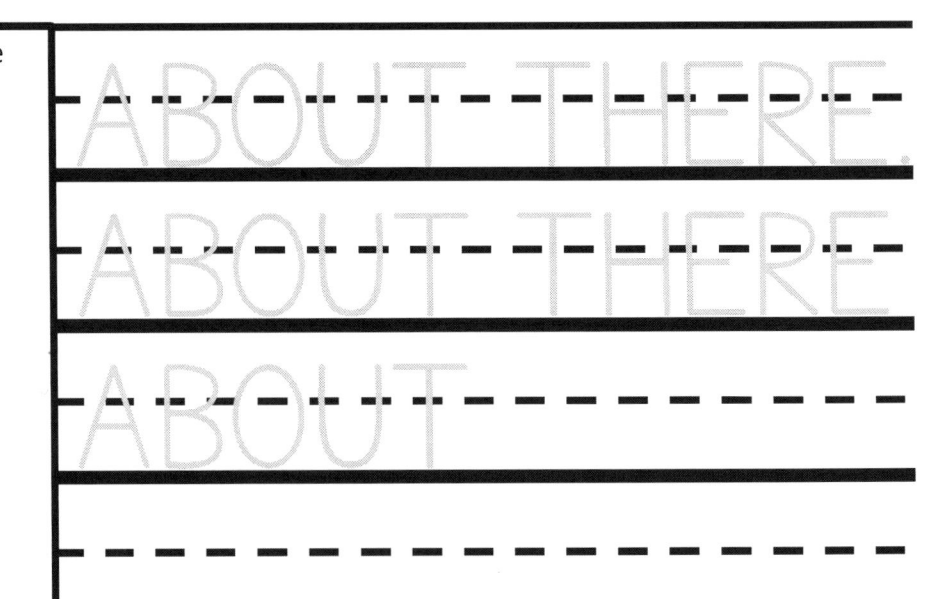

ABOUT

I LOVE TO LEARN ABOUT SCIENCE.

ABOUT   ABOUT

FIND AND TRACE THE WORD ABOUT

COULD   PLAY   SO
ABOUT   ABOUT   OUR
     ABOUT   A   TOO

ABOUT

Draw a picture of the sentence

ABOUT THERE.
ABOUT THERE
ABOUT

USE

I USE ALL THE CRAYONS.

USE   USE   USE

FIND AND TRACE THE WORD USE

BYE   USE   USE
COULD   USE   LIKE
LITTLE   USE   CAME

USE

Draw a picture of the sentence

USE RED NOW.
USE RED
USE

HIM

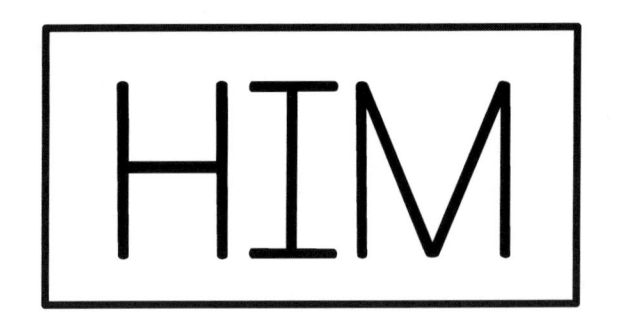

THAT GIFT IS FOR HIM.

HIM HIM HIM

FIND AND TRACE THE WORD HIM

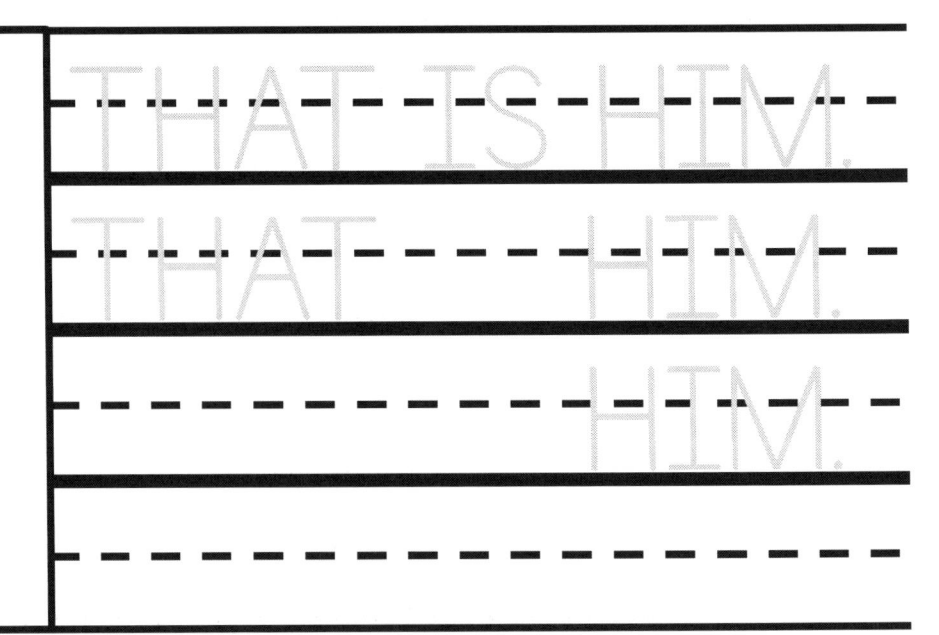

HIM HIM KNOW
FUNNY UNDER HIM
ONCE AGAIN HIM

HIM

Draw a picture of the sentence

THAT IS HIM.
THAT HIM.
HIM.

THEIR

IT WAS THEIR TURN.

THEIR   THEIR

FIND AND TRACE THE WORD THEIR

GET   HAD   THEIR
THEIR   AS   DID
     THEIR   THEIR
              HOW

THEIR

Draw a picture of the sentence

THEIR HAT!

THEIR HAT!

THEIR

OUT

I'LL GO OUT
THERE WITH YOU.

OUT   OUT   OUT

FIND AND TRACE THE WORD OUT

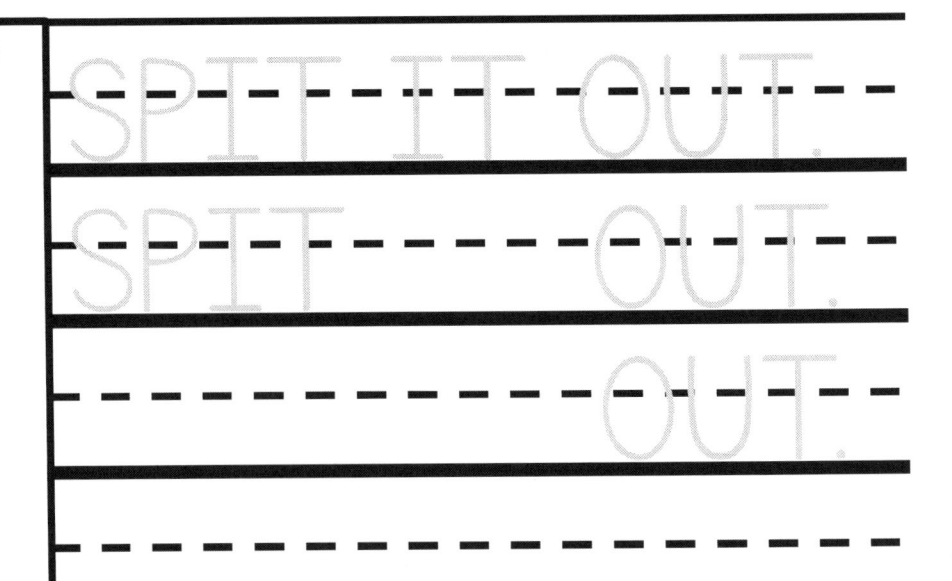

OUT   BY   OUT
SAID   OUT   WHAT
        BY   PUT   OUT

OUT

Draw a picture of the sentence

SPIT IT OUT.
SPIT IT OUT.
OUT.

THESE

THESE ARE SO FUN TO DO!

THESE   THESE

FIND AND TRACE THE WORD THESE

MAKE   THESE   THIS
IT   BUT
    ON   THESE
THESE   THESE

THESE

Draw a picture of the sentence

THESE GO UP.

THESE GO

THESE

BEEN

IT'S BEEN SO LONG SINCE I'VE SEEN YOU.

BEEN   BEEN

FIND AND TRACE THE WORD BEEN

HAD   BEEN   HAD
GET   HOW   BEEN
       BEEN
BEEN   DID

BEEN

Draw a picture of the sentence

BEEN THERE!
BEEN THERE
BEEN

IN

WILL YOU STAY IN WITH ME?

IN IN IN IN

FIND AND TRACE THE WORD IN

IN   OTHER   IN
WOULD   EACH   THAN
NOT   IN   IN

IN

Draw a picture of the sentence

IN THE MUG.
IN THE
IN

CAN

CAN YOU HEAR ME?

CAN   CAN   CAN

FIND AND TRACE THE WORD CAN

GOING   THEN   HAS
CAN   CAN   CAN
   CAN   JUST   HIS

CAN

Draw a picture of the sentence

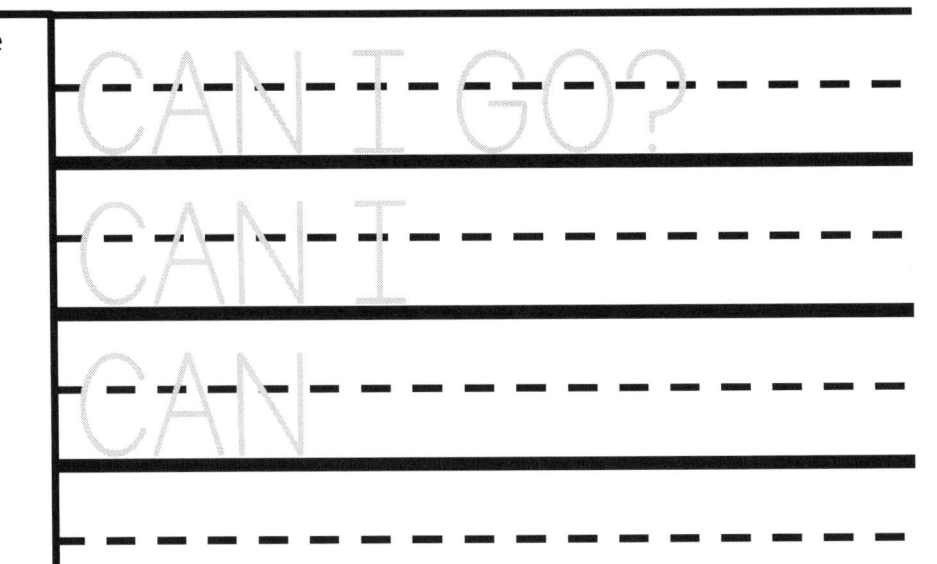

CAN I GO?
CAN I
CAN

REVIEW: Word Search

COPY EACH WORD IN THE WORD SEARCH THEN CROSS IT OFF IN THE WORD BANK

WORD BANK:

COULD	THEN	AGAIN	YOUR	EACH
EVERY	JUST	ONCE	MADE	GET
WHEN	KNOW	FUNNY	HOW	ABOUT
GOING	UNDER	SOME	MAKE	BEEN

```
Z  F  E  V  E  R  Y  U  A  T
C  U  H  O  W  Q  O  N  B  H
O  N  Y  B  H  U  U  D  O  E
U  N  V  E  E  V  R  E  U  N
L  Y  W  E  N  J  W  R  T  X
D  X  M  N  R  U  M  A  K  E
A  G  A  I  N  S  O  N  C  E
U  E  D  R  P  T  S  O  M  E
T  T  E  S  Q  K  N  O  W  Y
G  O  I  N  G  E  A  C  H  Z
```

Copyrighted Materials: All Rights Reserved
© Resource Teacher's Guide LLC 2023-present

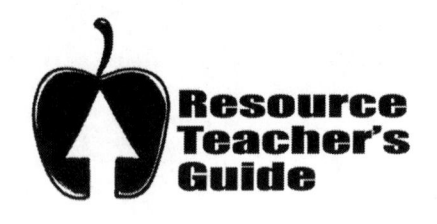

Terms Of Use

This product is the intellectual property of Resource Teacher's Guide all rights reserved, and may only be used for personal classroom use by one single teacher. This product may not be copied, modified, repackaged, resold, shared or distributed; this includes making copies for other teachers. You may purchase an additional license for a discounted price by going to "my purchases" and clicking "buy additional licenses". You may not copy any part of this product to place on personal websites, blogs, classroom websites, or district websites.

Find these worksheets in lower case letters as well!

Check out our Amazon store now!

www.resourceteachersguide.com

©Resource Teacher's Guide LLC2023-Present

Made in the USA
Columbia, SC
17 December 2023